PAST & PRESENT SCOTLAND
a new perspective

Since the Roman invasion of Scotland just after the birth of Christ, dominion over this most beautiful of countries has been the cause of fierce and bloody conflict. Centuries of struggle between the Scots and their longstanding English foes have time and time again shown the spirit of Scotland to be proudly independent and reflected as much in the wild and romantic Highland scenery as in its rough and bloodstained history.

In Past & Present Scotland the legendary battles and heroic figures, the traditions, the culture and the very essence of Scotland are brought together to give a new perspective on a remarkable people, their heritage and the unique nation that is Scotland today.

Past & Present Scotland

by Sarah Newitt

Cover Illustration   Liz Wright

Published in the United Kingdom
by Ptarmigan Publishing Ltd

Ptarmigan House
No 9 The Coda Centre
189 Munster Road
London SW6 6AW

Telephone: 0171-381 5600
Facsimile: 0171-381 4012

ISBN 0 9526380 6 1

British Library Cataloguing in Publication Data. A catalogue record for this book is available from the British Library.

Acknowledgements
John Hutchinson and Sue Hall at Still Moving Picture Company, National Galleries of Scotland, The Royal Collection Windsor, Scottish Record Office, HMSO, Simon Dawson, Jonathan Cottam, Gary McGovern, and Julia Peddie.

Contents

Scotland - a brief history

Although prehistoric sites show that Scotland was first colonised about six thousand years ago, the first inhabitants to be identified were the early Bronze Age Beaker People who arrived in the second millennium BC. They were ousted by the fugitive Celts a thousand years later, whose savagery, and determined resistance to Roman invasion from 80 AD onwards, led the hitherto victorious Romans to conclude that conquering Caledonia was probably not worth the trouble and man power involved. Adopting a defensive strategy, the Roman Emperor Hadrian built a wall between Scotland and England in 122 AD to defend his English territory against the marauding northerners, and by the end of the fourth century the Romans, their priorities elsewhere, had accepted the inevitable and, giving up all attempts to subdue Caledonia, abandoned it to the "barbarians".

Skara Brae
prehistoric Orkney dwellings

The Romans deserted Britain south of Hadrian's Wall in the fifth century, and in the ensuing Dark Ages the native Celtic Britons of England were driven into Scotland by Anglo Saxon invaders from across the North Sea. By the sixth century, Scotland was far from peacefully occupied by four disunited and aggressive races; the indigenous and powerful Celtic Picts, the Scots from Celtic Northern Ireland, the Teutonic Anglo Saxons from the Rhinelands and the Britons of England.

Hadrian's Wall

Although Christianity was not unknown in Scotland in Roman times, the task facing early Christian missionaries was a daunting one. St Ninian and the Irish St Columba were the first to tackle the pagan and volatile heathens and to the credit of those remarkable men and their apostles, the four Scottish kingdoms were ostensibly Christian by the end of the seventh century, albeit politically very separate and unaligned for some time with the Church of Rome.

In fact it was not until the ninth century that any political unity did exist. Kenneth MacAlpin, the canny King of the Scots, seized the Pictish throne while the Picts were in disarray following a fracas with the Vikings. The Anglo Saxons, who had settled Lothian, and the Britons, who had settled Strathclyde, remained independent until much later, which was no doubt due in part to the time and energy Kenneth's successors were forced to spend defending themselves against Viking raiders, who had been causing havoc since the end of the eighth century and who controlled Orkney, Shetland and the Western Isles by the end of the ninth century.

Scotland, bar the Viking holdings, was fully united under one monarch only when King Duncan, whose grandfather had conquered the Angles, inherited the throne of the Britons on slightly tenuous grounds in 1034. His brief reign was terminated by Macbeth, who dispatched him in battle somewhat less treacherously than Shakespeare would have it, although posthumous revenge was exacted when Duncan's son Malcolm III returned the compliment and murdered Macbeth, thereby regaining his family's throne.

Malcolm was not only anglicised, having been brought up in England, but married to one of the many English aristocrats taking refuge in the Scottish Lowlands after the Norman invasion in 1066. Under Margaret's influence celibacy, poverty and other unpopular English practices were imposed on an appalled clergy and the seeds of an Episcopal system introduced to the Church. The focus of an increasingly anglicised court life shifted to the Anglo Saxon Lowlands, causing a bitter rift with the Celtic Highlands that was to shape Scottish history for centuries.

Malcolm, despite his links with the English court, was not without an acquisitive eye to his southern neighbour. During one of several border raids he was killed and succeeded by a chaotic series of weak kings, until his ninth son, David I, came to the throne in 1124. David's English upbringing manifested itself in several ways: feudalism - land in return for pledged loyalty and service, in marked contrast to the patriarchal system of the Highland clans - was introduced to the Lowlands, Scottish estates were distributed among prominent Anglo Normans and control of the flourishing Church entrusted to Norman prelates. This was all to lead to trouble, but in the short term the great administrative improvements David introduced had an enormously beneficial effect on life in Scotland, particularly in the Lowlands.

Two ineffectual monarchs later, William the Lion signed a pact with the French, which was to become the longstanding "Auld Alliance", and then followed the best of Scottish traditions by invading England in 1174. He was catastrophically defeated and forced to swear fealty to Henry II, a humiliation which lasted until the end of the twelfth century when Richard the Lionheart removed his troops and renounced feudal rights over Scotland in return for crusade funds.

Meanwhile, the rebellious Chieftains of Western Scotland and the Highlands, who adamantly refused to acknowledge even the concept of a central Scottish monarchy, were in their usual state of insurrection. William's son and grandson, Alexanders II and III, turned their respective attentions to subduing the Celts and in particular the Lords of the Western Isles, whose allegiance still lay with the Norwegians. This so incensed King Hakon of Norway that he declared war on Scotland and in the

Stirling Castle

following Battle of Largs victory for the Scots led to the return of the Hebrides (otherwise known as The Western Isles) in 1266.

Two judicious marriages followed, fostering temporary peace with England and lasting peace and friendship with Norway. Alexander III married Margaret, daughter of Henry III, and their daughter married the reigning Norwegian king, thereby concluding four hundred years of bloody conflict. The ensuing period of calm and prosperity was, however, short-lived and came to an abrupt end when, on Alexander's death in 1286, his young Norwegian granddaughter became Queen of Scotland.

Edward I Plantaganet of England, seeing the Scottish throne within reach, immediately arranged a match between his son and the infant Queen. His intentions became clear when, despite assurances that Scotland would remain independent, he moved for English troops to be stationed in southern Scotland. Scottish sensibilities were suitably outraged, but the immediate crisis was resolved when the Queen was drowned en route to Britain, and the question of the

Stirling Bridge
and the Wallace monument

succession became paramount. Thirteen claimants and an interfering and predatory English king were a volatile combination which led to a dispute prompting decades of conflict between Scotland and England.

At the behest of the Norman Bishop of St Andrews, Edward was invited to choose the successor and after nominal deliberation elected John Balliol on the grounds of his amenability to English control. Although a weak spirit, even Balliol rebelled at Edward's demands for, amongst other things, feudal superiority over Scotland and contributions to English defence costs. So, after reaffirming the Auld Alliance with France, he invaded England. Edward, "the Hammer of the Scots", retaliated by rampaging through Scotland, defeating Balliol, and in 1296 declared himself King of Scotland. Taking the Crowning Stone of the Scottish Kings, the "Stone of Scone" to London, he left in return English officials and soldiers to run the country.

The following spring, one William Wallace scuffled with some English soldiers in Lanarck. He escaped, but his female accomplice was captured and put to death by the Sheriff, whom Wallace killed in revenge. Immediately outlawed, he became the catalyst for an explosion of nationalist feeling, the zenith of which was a decisive victory over a large English army at Stirling Bridge in 1297. His luck ran out the next summer when he was crushingly defeated by Edward at Falkirk, and although for seven years he eluded capture while Edward's army devastated Scotland, he was eventually caught and most brutally executed. His quartered remains were distributed to Newcastle, Berwick, Stirling and Perth to discourage others harbouring ideas of revolt.

But there were others, including several disaffected nobles of Norman descent whose allegiance had until then been to the English crown. Of them, Robert de Brus (the Bruce) and John Comyn, who were both technically claimants to the throne, were rival leaders and in 1306 Bruce took the initiative, disposed of the competition and had himself crowned King on Palm Sunday at Scone Palace. The fact that he had stabbed Comyn in a kirk was, however, not insignificant. Not only was he excommunicated for several years, but at the same time he had also brought the wrath of the powerful Comyns upon himself.

Almost immediately after his coronation Bruce was defeated and forced into exile by Edward I, and it was not until nearly a year later that he was able to return to a ravaged Scotland and rally support. The military tide turned against the English and on Edward's death Bruce went from strength to strength, subduing the Comyns and their allies, convening Scotland's first parliament, gaining the support of the Scottish Church, despite his excommunication, and finally recovering all the lands lost to Edward I, bar Stirling. When Edward's son, Edward II, finally felt obliged to help this last beleaguered garrison in 1314, he encountered Bruce's army at Bannockburn just below the town. Edward's men were well equipped, and there were three times as many of them as there were Scots, but Bruce was on familiar territory. He forced the enemy into the marshes, and in one of Scotland's historic triumphs, routed them utterly - thereby securing not only his crown, but also his status as a national hero.

Edward's subsequent attempt at troublemaking, having failed so conspicuously in wordly and military matters, was to ask the Pope to reconfirm Bruce's excommunication. This backfired badly, eliciting a furious reaction from the Scottish Church and nobles in the form of the Declaration of Arbroath, one of the greatest affirmations of national intent ever written, in which Scotland vehemently rejected the interference of Rome and declared her independence from England.

In the face of such conviction the Pope eventually annulled Bruce's excommunication and recognised him as legitimate King in 1324. The English followed suit in 1328, when a Peace Treaty between Scotland and a war-weary England acknowledged Scotland as an independent country and Bruce as her King. When he died a year later Scotland was relatively stable, united for the first time by a strong feeling of nationalism, even to the inclusion of the Celtic Highlanders who had fought alongside Bruce against the English at Bannockburn.

His son David II's reign was marked by political machination and chicanery, excessive even by the standards of those days. Much of the mischief was generated by Edward III, intent on re-establishing English influence in Scotland. However he was soon distracted by the Hundred Years War with France, which took direct pressure off Scotland, but also meant that in honouring the Auld Alliance, campaigns requested by the French to "divert" English forces by invading England were mounted more than once. During the first, David was captured and held, to his delight, at the civilised English court. After the second, Edward changed tack and hit upon the idea of crippling Scotland financially by ransoming David back to the Scots for a staggering 100,000 marks.

As a means of subordinating Scotland it was certainly successful, especially given the simultaneous floods, plague and resulting demoralisation. In fact, so successful a strategy was it that David's reign ended with an ignominious private arrangement to surrender sovereignty to the English, which was predictably rejected out of hand by the Scottish Parliament. So it was that on David's death in 1371 the throne passed to Bruce's daughter's son Robert Stewart, whose father's family (hence the name, later changed to Stuart by Mary Queen of Scots) were Hereditary High Stewards of Scotland.

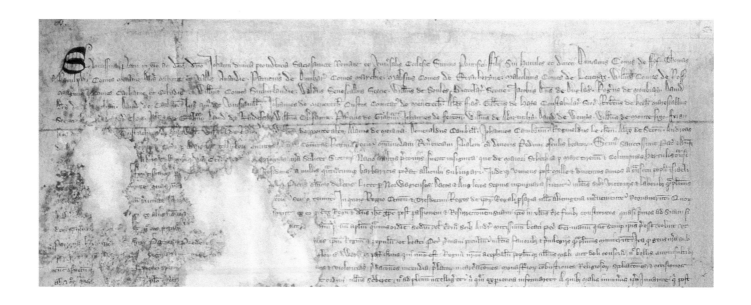

Although the Wars of Independence with England were over, peace still eluded Scotland. Internal strife between the unruly nobility and the Crown was a constant threat to the authority of the monarchy for centuries and under the early Stewart kings royal power declined and Scotland degenerated into a rough and lawless society.

By the time Robert II's grandson, James I, was heir to the throne, the turbulence within Scotland was severe enough to warrant his exile for safekeeping. By mischance in 1406 he was taken prisoner by the English on his way to France and spent eighteen years in captivity, during which time the Scottish nobles took every opportunity to increase their power whilst studiously ignoring the plight of their King.

By 1424 the situation between England and Scotland was relatively calm. James was engaged to the English King's cousin, and after a shattering defeat at Scottish hands in France (the Auld Alliance again), England was keen to make peace with Scotland. James was ransomed back to the Scots and he returned to a country in the grip of outright anarchy. Retribution was swift. James was not only intelligent and well educated; he also bitterly resented the conspicuous lack of effort to secure his release while in captivity. He ruthlessly imposed his authority over the Highland and Lowland nobles, whom he treated with some harshness, and introduced a necessary if unpopular programme of reforms. His treatment of the nobility earned him their hatred, and in 1437 he was stabbed to death in front of his horrified English wife.

"To the Most Holy Father in Christ and Lord, the Lord John, by divine providence supreme Pontiff of the Holy Roman and Universal Church, his devout sons Douglas, Earl of Fife ..."

The earls and barons of Scotland petition the Pope during War of Independence through the Declaration of Arbroath

*James III with St Andrew
and Prince James*

from The Trinity Altarpiece
by Hugo van der Goes c1478

James II came to the throne as a minor, as did every Scottish monarch for the next two hundred years. Scheming Regents and rapacious nobles notwithstanding, he extended royal control over the dissident factions and continued his father's reforms. He was a popular and civilised King, but one who did not baulk at brutal measures. Twice during his reign the threatening and overpowerful Douglases were brought into line by the cold-blooded murder of the Earl of the day over dinner in a royal palace.

James III was a different character altogether, his only contribution to Scottish history being the return of the Orkneys and Shetlands following his marriage to the King of Norway's daughter. However his son, yet another James, finally broke the somewhat unprepossessing Stewart mould. Known as the glittering and tragic Renaissance King, his charm and flamboyance endeared him to the common people while his intellect and devoutness were an inspiration to those around him. During his reign, the arts, learning and culture flourished and life in Scotland acquired a considerable degree of sophistication and civilisation.

In 1502 he signed the Eternal Treaty, "a good, real, sincere, true, entire and firm peace, bond, league and confederation on land and sea, to endure for ever" with Henry VII of England, and in 1503 he married Margaret Tudor, Henry's daughter. For several years, he brokered amicable relations between the English and the French, but when England joined the Papacy, Spain and Venice against France, James remained loyal to his old allies and marched on England. Scottish and English armies met at Flodden and thereafter followed Scotland's worst defeat at English hands; a massacre in which not only was the King killed, but the flower of Scottish nobility too. In all 12,000 Scots perished on that September day in 1513.

Thirteen years of chaos and intrigue ensued while the heir, James V, was still an infant. Nonetheless, by the time James assumed the mantle of King aged fourteen, Scotland was deemed an important player in the European scene, and her allegiance a prize worth having. Henry VIII of England had broken with the Catholic Church in 1534 and offered James his daughter in marriage, hoping to enrol him in his anti-Catholic campaign, while the Holy Roman Emperor and even the Pope sought to find a wife for him. In the end, to Henry's disgust, James declared his Catholic and French loyalties by marrying first the daughter of the King of France and, on her death, Marie of Guise. Henry was determined to win Scotland over to his new Protestantism and in 1542 declared himself Lord Superior of Scotland. During the unavoidable clash that followed, James' half-hearted army was defeated and he died of ill health and, so the story goes, disappointment on hearing that his new born babe was female.

Mary, of course, was no ordinary female. Crowned Queen of Scots at one week old in 1542, she became the focus of Henry's designs on Scotland. Plans for a match between his son and Mary violently rejected, he adopted a more direct approach and reduced Edinburgh and the Borders to rubble in the "Rough Wooing", engendering a bitter loathing for the English that was to last for centuries.

Meanwhile, the corrupt and wealthy Catholic church in Scotland was losing credibility. Throughout Europe the Protestant reforms of Luther, Zwingli and Calvin were gaining popularity and in view of England's religious, albeit political, volte face, the Scottish Catholic Church was understandably nervous. But illegal English Bibles were filtering into Scotland and the effect was dramatic and irreversible. Reformation became inevitable as people realised that Christianity was not exclusively bound up with the Catholicism of the elite.

The Protestants were, not surprisingly, viciously persecuted and after their first martyr, Patrick Hamilton, was burnt at the stake in 1528 many of their leaders fled the country. Two of the first to return were George Wishart and the eloquent but gravely serious John Knox, who braved the perils of a Scotland under the Queen Mother's French Catholic influence in 1544. For their pains, Wishart was arrested then burnt at the stake and Knox taken hostage by the French to be a galley slave. In 1549 he was released, unbowed by two years' hard labour, and settled in Geneva where he was profoundly influenced by Calvin. In 1555 he returned to Scotland, galvanising the Protestant movement with his mesmerising rhetoric, and two years later the First Covenant was drawn up uniting Scottish Protestants and urging them to forsake the Catholic "Congregation of Satan".

John Knox
wood engraving
after a portrait by Adrian Vanson

At this juncture Mary married the French Dauphin and with the news that she had bequeathed Scotland to France in the event of her death without heir, the spectre of becoming a province of Catholic France gripped the nation. Knox's exhortations tipped the balance and violent anti-French and anti-Catholic riots spread through Scotland. Scottish fears proved well founded when Mary's husband came to the French throne and immediately quartered his arms with not only those of Scotland, but England too. Deeming the new Protestant Queen, Elizabeth I, technically illegitimate due to her father's heresy, Francois believed his wife to be rightful claimant to the English throne.

Elizabeth therefore had more than a vested interest in helping the Scottish Protestants. Disapproving of rebel tactics, and particularly unenamoured of the misogynist Knox, she nonetheless appreciated the need for a united front against the French, and accordingly in 1560 an English fleet fell upon French forces supporting the Queen Mother in Scotland. Later that year Marie of Guise died and the Auld Alliance with her. Elizabeth I was formally recognised as Queen of England, English and French troops withdrew from Scotland, and a new chapter in Scottish history began.

Shortly afterwards a Reformation Parliament outlawed Mass and denied the Pope's authority, further crippling the Catholic church in Scotland. An austere Calvinist Presbyterian Kirk evolved,

Mary Queen of Scots
by an unknown artist
after her death

governed by Presbyteries of elders in contrast to the bishop controlled Episcopal church. The General Assembly of the Kirk was set up to deal with church affairs, and subsequently expanded its remit to became the forum for general debate that it is today. The austerity, high moral standards, independence and distrust of state authority that characterised Calvinism became the enduring basis for Scottish life, and the importance attached to education and learning was to have far reaching effects on the intellectual contribution Scotland was to make in future generations.

Protestantism had prevailed, although in a joyless and severe form, and it was to a joyless and severe Scotland that the vivacious, hot blooded and available Mary returned after her husband's death in 1560. Although staunchly Catholic, Mary wisely chose not to impose her faith on the Scots, who were deeply disapproving of her frivolity and became even more so as they watched the charade of her marital life unfold. Mary's judgement in choosing husbands was abysmal; number two was the Catholic and worthless Lord Darnley, who stabbed her Italian secretary to death in a jealous rage and was later found strangled. Charming, Protestant and probably heavily involved in Darnley's murder, Earl Bothwell quickly divorced his wife to become Mary's next husband, but this time she had gone too far. Scotland was outraged by her behaviour and she was abducted, paraded through the streets in a harlot's petticoat and forced to relinquish her throne. Her one year old son by Darnley was crowned James VI and Mary escaped to England in 1568, where she was imprisoned by Elizabeth and eventually beheaded on a trumped-up charge twenty years later.

Years of turmoil followed Mary's flight. James' Regents were murdered, political intrigue abounded, plots for Catholic risings were hatched and it was not until 1582 when James was kidnapped by Protestant nobles who subsequently took control of the country that there was any degree of stability in Scotland. At seventeen, James escaped and declared himself King. Despite a penchant for favourites and an obsession with witchcraft, he proved an intelligent and cultured monarch, although his reign was disrupted by the usual antagonisms between nobility and Crown as well as religious confrontations.

James was ambitious as well as intelligent, and keeping on the right side of his cousin Elizabeth I, the "Virgin Queen", in the hope of inheriting the English crown on her death was a high priority. Only murmuring dissent when his mother was beheaded, his policy paid dividends and in 1603 he became the first King of Scotland and England.

Despite being an avowed Protestant, James was strongly opposed to the Presbyterian principles of church government by assembly and the growing extremism of the Kirk, which Knox's successor, Andrew Melville, believed had divine authority to direct civil affairs. James not only wanted to control the powerful church through a hierarchy of bishops appointed by and answerable to him but furiously resented any interference by the church in his own Divine Right to run state affairs as he and he alone saw fit.

Mary Queen of Scots House
near Jedburgh
reputedly the location for romantic
assignations in the Borders, now a
museum dedicated to her memory

As a result, he reintroduced the Episcopacy, banned the General Assembly from meeting, and on his first and only visit to Scotland after becoming King of England further alienated the Scots by forcing through the deeply unpopular Five Articles which espoused much higher church practices than were acceptable in Scotland, such as the observation of Christian festivals and receiving of Holy Communion on bended knee.

James was also determined to pacify the Highlands and reassert Crown authority over the dissident Scottish nobility. This he did by quite ruthlessly playing the clans off against each other and taking fearsome action against offenders, in particular the MacGregors who were henceforth forbidden even to use their family name.

When James died in 1625, he left a rich legacy. Under his auspices the King James Version of the Bible was published, the foundation stones of the British Empire laid and some of Shakespeare's finest plays written. His heir however was emphatically not of the same calibre. A stranger to Scotland, Charles I knew little and understood less of the political and religious issues at stake in either Scotland or England and believed as implicitly as his father in the Divine Right of Kings, specifically his own. It was a disastrous state of affairs that was ultimately to lead to the English Civil War.

His first major error was in trying to bring the Scottish Kirk into line with the English Church by foisting the Anglican and Episcopalian practices of his own faith on the Scots. But this paled into insignificance in comparison with his extraordinarily ill-judged attempt in 1637 to introduce a Revised Prayer Book for Scotland. Charles and Archbishop Laud had recognised that the English Prayer Book would never be acceptable to the Scots, but what they had failed to appreciate was the total antipathy of the Presbyterians to any form of liturgy given their attachment to extemporary prayer.

The reaction in Scotland was violent and unequivocal and culminated in the creation of the National Covenant, a pledge to maintain the "true" religion of Scotland. The religious fervour that now swept through the country, the resentment of Charles' absenteeism and anglophilia and ever growing feelings of nationalism were an explosive combination. Unnerved, Charles agreed to a meeting of the disempowered General Assembly but then dismissed its decisions as invalid. It was the final straw for the Scots.

In the Bishops' Wars that followed, Charles was defeated twice, and forced to agree to the demands of the Covenanters for a free Assembly and Parliament. But war was an expensive pastime and when Charles ran out of money, he had no option but to summon his English Parliament, without whose services he had seen fit to govern for the past ten years. His chief supporters were immediately executed and in 1642 the Civil War broke out between Charles' Catholic Royalists and the Puritan Parliamentarians.

Scotland was eventually persuaded to join the fray under the bizarre Solemn League and Covenant which traded Scottish military support for the Parliamentarians for £30,000 a month and the assurance that England would in future embrace Presbyterianism. Charles was defeated by Cromwell and in 1643 surrendered to the Scots who, having entered the war for theological rather than political reasons, ransomed him back to the English for £40,000. Shortly afterwards he was beheaded, to the perverse horror of his Scottish subjects who were outraged at the English for executing their monarch.

__The Crown of Scotland__
now on permanent display
in Edinburgh Castle

His son, Charles II, was offered the Scottish crown, although only on condition of signing the Covenant, which he accepted, prompting Cromwell immediately to go on the offensive again. After several defeats the Scots had no option but to surrender. The King fled to exile in France, Parliament was abolished and Scotland became an occupied country.

Under Cromwell as Lord High Protector and his unpopular but efficient regime, life in Scotland as part of the Commonwealth was peaceful, if austere. On Cromwell's death in 1659, Charles returned from France restoring not only the united monarchy and the Scottish Parliament, but also the turmoil of the pre-Cromwell years. By filling his new Parliament with Royalists, he secured absolute power for himself and, totally disregarding the Covenant he had signed on his succession, declared that "Presbytery was not a religion for gentlemen". He reinstated the Episcopacy and removed much of the power of the Kirk, provoking such violent opposition that dissenting ministers abandoned their churches and held unauthorised services in the open air. The religious rebels were again mercilessly persecuted and although the Covenanters in true Calvinist spirit probably took a certain grim satisfaction from their plight, the 1680s became known, with good reason, as the Killing Time.

Charles was succeeded by his Catholic brother James VII of Scotland and II of England in 1685. He immediately made himself universally unpopular by decreeing religious freedom for all denominations and the arrival of his heir, and thus the increasing likelihood of a Catholic succession, precipitated the Glorious Revolution in which William of Orange, James' Dutch son-in-law, was invited to invade England and overthrow the King. James fled to Ireland and in 1689 William and Mary were crowned King and Queen of England, Ireland, and Scotland.

But James still had support in the Highlands and these Jacobites, as they were known, were feisty and courageous protagonists. Under Graham of Claverhouse they made a heroic stand against William's troops, and it was only after several savage encounters in Scotland and the Battle of the Boyne in Ireland that the Jacobites finally accepted defeat and James gave up any hope of regaining his throne.

Glencoe *site of the massacre of the Campbells in 1692*

William was fully aware of the problems brewing in Scotland. He ordered an English garrison to be built at Fort William and offered a pardon to all Jacobites who would swear allegiance to him before New Year's Day in 1692. The MacDonalds missed the deadline by a few days and William then perpetrated an appalling injustice as a show of strength. The Campbells were commanded to lodge with the MacDonalds at Glencoe and in the dead of night put every clan member under 70 to death. It was one of the most distasteful and shameful episodes in Scottish history and one which won him no friends in Scotland or England.

As William became more unpopular in Scotland, so relations with England deteriorated to a level of violent antipathy. Although a Protestant, he was distrusted by Episcopalians and Presbyterians alike, and under his influence free trade was increasingly obstructed in favour of the English. Additionally he was held largely to blame for the failure of an overseas venture, the Darien Project, which had cost thousands of Scottish lives and hundreds of thousands of Scottish pounds.

Against this very unlikely backdrop, William mooted the possibility of a union between the two countries just before he died. When Queen Anne, daughter of the deposed James II, came to the throne in 1702 and failed to produce an heir, there were enough bargaining tools on each side to conclude a Treaty of Union. The Protestant English were appalled at the prospect of a Stuart restoration through James' son, and it was this that gave the Scots their negotiating power.

Predictably, the wrangling was bitter and acrimonious, but in 1707 the Treaty was signed and Great Britain came into existence. Scotland agreed to a Hanoverian succession through the distaff descendants of James VI and I in return for trade concessions. Demands for an independent Parliament were rejected outright on the grounds that Scotland's gain in commercial equality with England far exceeded any rights to federalism, so Scottish representation at Parliament was left in the hands of 16 peers and 45 MPs. The legal system and Scottish Church were untouched and Scotland received nearly £400,000 in part for taking on some of England's debt and in part as compensation for the Darian Project. As the Jacobites said, "We are bought and sold for English gold."

Not surprisingly, strife followed almost immediately. Although the Union had been agreed with Scotland's economic interests at heart, it was hardly a popular move. English taxes, and particularly those on the widely-drunk French claret, were enormously unpopular, Scottish interests were neglected at the single Parliament and the Presbyterians were far from convinced of their own security under the new regime. As Daniel Defoe said, "I never saw a nation so universally wild ... it seems a perfect gangrene of the temper."

No wonder then that the Jacobites who, in common with Louis XIV of France, had recognised James II's son as King were fired with enthusiasm for a Stuart restoration. When the unappealing George I of Hanover came to the throne in 1714, James Edward, the Old Pretender, called on the Earl of Mar to raise the clans. In September 1715 he was declared King James VIII and III of Scotland and England in Braemar, but Mar was militarily incompetent and after the uninspiring James abandoned his men and slipped away into the night, his ill-led and dispirited Jacobite army was quashed by a force a quarter its size.

English retribution was brutal, and with anti-Union feeling running higher than ever, the Jacobites rose again in 1719, this time with Spanish backing. But the campaign was no more successful than previous attempts. Bad luck dogged them and the Government, persevering in its quest to subdue the Scots, passed an Act of Parliament forbidding the carrying of arms in public, opened up the previously inaccessible Highlands with a huge network of roads and bridges built under the auspices of General Wade to link his garrisons, and raised what was to become the Black Watch Regiment as a policing force.

By 1745 England was at war with France and the Old Pretender's son, the romantically nicknamed Bonnie Prince Charlie, saw a chance to reclaim his father's crown. Although French support for his cause was unexpectedly lukewarm he raised money by pawning family jewels and set sail for Scotland where, notwithstanding Scottish resentment of the ever unpopular House of Hanover and the high handed behaviour of the English, his reception was also unexpectedly unenthusiastic.

Garvamore Bridge on the Spey

constructed by Wade to improve military access to the Highlands

Rallying what support he could, the Young Pretender marched south, proclaimed his father King James VIII and III for the second time, and gathering largely Highland reinforcements advanced into England to seize the English crown. Charles reached Derby with little difficulty (helped no doubt by the widespread conviction that the Highlanders were cannibals) and causing such panic in London that the king prepared to leave the country; but here his resolve failed and pursued by two Hanoverian armies, he fled to Scotland.

The following April on Drumossie Moor near Culloden, Charles's hungry, ill-equipped Highland army was massacred in a matter of minutes by the "Butcher" Duke of Cumberland's far superior troops. The Prince escaped to the Isle of Skye dressed as Flora MacDonald's maid and, from the same place at which he had landed just over a year beforehand, sailed to permanent exile in Italy.

After Culloden the Government spared no effort to crush the Highlanders and persecute the remaining Jacobites. A concerted effort was made to break up the clan system and the Disarming Act banned playing bagpipes, on the grounds that they were instruments of war, carrying or even possessing weapons and wearing plaid or tartan in any form. Spoken Gaelic had been prohibited since 1695, and with the abolition of the inherited status of the clan chiefs and the virtual annihilation of the Highland way of life, there followed a great exodus of Scots to all corners of the world.

Had Bonnie Prince Charles been Protestant, Scottish history would no doubt have been very different. As it was he died a sad alcoholic in a rented Italian palace, still styling himself Charles III. His brother, the last remaining Stuart, entered the Church thereby sealing the fate of his family. With his death in 1807 came the end of the Stuart dynasty and Scottish claim to the throne.

Thereafter the history of Scotland became largely inseparable from that of England and many of the same influences and causes bound the two countries together. As in England, the industrial revolution of the eighteenth and nineteenth centuries irrevocably altered the social and economic structure of Scotland. The rural economy of central Scotland changed to one based initially on a flourishing textile industry and then in the nineteenth century on world class heavy engineering and shipbuilding industries. Coal, steel and fishing boomed and demands for labour concentrated the population in towns and around industrial centres, also attracting large numbers of Irish immigrants fleeing the potato famine in Ireland. Canals, bridges and roads were built and, after Watt's invention of the steam engine in the 1840s, an extensive railway network further improved communications. Although working conditions and wages were appalling by today's standards, the benefits of industrialisation in southern Scotland were widespread.

This was, however, not the case in the Highlands. The demise of the clan system and its patriarchal obligations after the '45 Rebellion had reduced many of the Highland Chiefs to the status of landlord. The agricultural revolution had improved farming methods and not only did increased food production and the

A Highland Chieftain c1680

*Painted by John Michael Wright,
the unidentified laird wears the dress
prohibited by the Disarming Act*

introduction of the easily grown and nutritious potato cause a minor population
explosion to levels unsustainable in the Highlands, but the economic benefits of
sheep farming rather than traditional crofting were indisputable. By the late

eighteenth century, some Highlanders had moved to the already overcrowded towns or overseas, but this voluntary drift was followed by the notorious Highland Clearances during which great tracts of land were cleared for sheep by the compulsory and often brutal eviction of tenants and destruction of their farms. The Clearances, Sutherland and Glengarry being particularly savage, lasted until the mid nineteenth century and prompted thousands to emigrate, many to America and Canada, rather than settle on the coast.

Meanwhile, intellectually and artistically Scotland was flourishing. The Enlightenment was a period of extraordinary creativity and by the end of the eighteenth century, Scotland, and specifically Edinburgh, was one of the major centres of European thinking and culture. Scottish economists, philosophers, architects, artists and writers were at the forefront of their fields and their output was as much responsible for Scotland's growing popularity in England and Europe as Queen Victoria's enthusiastic patronage. The Scots of the time were also intrepid explorers and missionaries, inventors and engineers and their contribution to the building of the British Empire and the New World was unparallelled.

During the first half of the nineteenth century a myriad of influences forged ever stronger links between Scotland and England and it was not until 1853 that any significant mention of Home Rule was made. By the beginning of the twentieth century, Scotland was one of the most prosperous countries in the world but the outbreak of World War 1, in which Scotland lost proportionately more men than any other part of the United Kingdom, halted the momentum and the economic slump that followed led to depression, unemployment and another spate of emigration. Many Scots felt the blame was due to neglect by the Government and the move for Home Rule was revived. The Scottish National Party was formed in 1934 to spearhead the campaign for political independence and, after the Second World War, a Covenant calling for a Scottish Parliament within the United Kingdom was signed by two million Scots. In 1950, the Crowning Stone of Scone, symbol of Scottish nationalism, was audaciously taken from Westminster and triumphantly albeit temporarily brought home, and by 1977 a Scottish

Devolution Bill had been approved by Parliament. The first Referendum on the Bill was inconclusive, but Margaret Thatcher's unpopular right wing policies galvanised the Home Rule advocates into action. In 1989 the Scottish Constitutional Convention produced a blueprint for a Scottish Parliament which was supported by fifty eight of Scotland's seventy two Parliamentary seats but dismissed by the Conservative Government. Eight years later the Scots voted overwhelmingly for their own Parliament, the first for nearly three hundred years, in an affirmation of the proud and independent spirit that has endured throughout Scottish history.

The Old Royal High School Edinburgh

one of the sites proposed for the Scottish Parliament

Scotland today

There can be few countries of its size in the world which afford the diversity of natural environments to be found in Scotland. From endless estuarine mudflats to towering cliffs, from lush lowland river and pasture to the harsh majesty of mountain peaks, it is a land of contrast and surprise.

Over the centuries, Scotland's inhabitants have left an equally varied and indelible mark on their land. From isolated Highland communities to the bustling cities built by industry, commerce, and unflagging optimism, a vivid sense of national character is expressed.

The following pages take a closer look at Scotland region by region, examining principal points of interest and highlighting major events, and provide an insight into some of the natural and cultural forces which continue to define the character of Scotland.

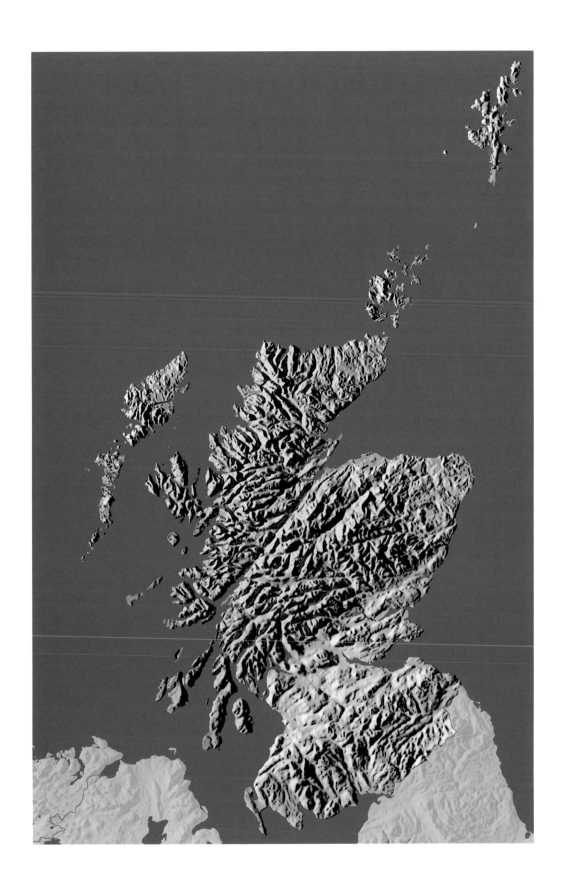

Edinburgh and the Lothians

Edinburgh is a strikingly beautiful city in a setting few places in the world can rival. Built on a series of extinct volcanoes and overlooking the Firth of Forth, Robert Louis Stevenson commented that "No situation could be more commanding for the head of a Kingdom, none better chosen for noble prospects."

The origin of the name Edinburgh is much disputed, and although Ptolemy wrote of a town called Dunedin in 160AD legend has it that Edinburgh either takes its name from a Pictish fortress built on Castle Rock called Dun Eidyn or, more popularly, from the Angle King Edwin who captured the town in the sixth century.

Castle Rock, a high volcanic plug surrounded by precipitous rockfaces on three sides, is an ideal natural site for a fortress and Edinburgh's history is inextricably linked to the castle's strategic importance. Edinburgh was Scotland's southern outpost until Malcolm III extended his Kingdom to the banks of the Tweed in 1018. Too close even then to the border for comfort, Edinburgh was sacked seven times by the English before the seventeenth century, but nonetheless during Malcolm's reign the newly built castle became a focus of court life. In the twelfth century a town developed around the foot of Castle Rock and eventually in the fifteenth century Edinburgh became the official capital of Scotland.

Under James IV early sixteenth century Edinburgh enjoyed a short but glittering Renaissance and, despite the turbulence surrounding the reign of Mary Queen of Scots and the Reformation, continued to prosper during the rest of the century. The University was founded in 1582 and established a reputation for excellence that spread as far afield as Russia; Tsar Peter the Great's doctors were nearly all trained in Edinburgh. Even after losing the Scottish court to London after the Union of Crowns in 1603, and the Scottish Parliament in 1707, Edinburgh remained the centre of the Scottish legal system and the Church of Scotland, and by the eighteenth century had become a formidable centre of learning and the arts.

Edinburgh Castle *from Grassmarket*

The New Town
from the air
model of Georgian
town planning

The Age of Enlightenment, as this period became known, propelled Edinburgh to European cultural and intellectual prominence and the creation of the New Town, a neoclassical masterpiece, prompted Edinburgh to be nicknamed the "Athens of the North".

During the nineteenth century Edinburgh's population quadrupled and Victorian suburbs spread into the surrounding areas. Whilst remaining prominent in the medical sciences, Edinburgh's importance as a cultural centre waned somewhat until the first International Festival in 1947, which has since become the world's largest arts festival and fully restored Edinburgh's status in the cultural world.

Physically, Edinburgh is a city of great contrasts. The tiny mediaeval Old Town, clustered below the steep cliffs of Castle Rock, is an atmospheric labyrinth of narrow twisting alleys. First enclosed in 1450, laws governing the growth of walled cities forced the inhabitants to build upwards, until buildings fifteen or sixteen stories high were commonplace. The overcrowding and lack of sanitation led to Edinburgh being known as "Auld Reekie" and in the eighteenth century the formidable Edinburgh Mob, a people's force led by the cobbler "General" Smith, held sway and administered rough justice when needed.

Dominating the Old Town, Edinburgh Castle has had a chequered history. All but destroyed by Robert the Bruce in the fourteenth century, it has been a royal residence, strategic pawn, prisoner of war camp and ordnance factory as well as witnessing the birth of James VI, the first King of Scotland and England. After the demise of the Stuart line and the Treaty of Union, the Scottish Crown Jewels were hidden in the castle for safekeeping and mislaid for over a century until Sir Walter Scott set up a commission to find them in 1818.

Along the "Royal Mile", so called as it links the castle with the Palace of Holyroodhouse, is a small Close named after Francis Brodie, whose schizophrenic criminal son was the inspiration for Stevenson's Dr Jekyll and Mr Hyde and who met his death on the gallows he designed himself. Further on, the High Kirk of St Giles, often miscalled St Giles' Cathedral, was the launchpad of John Knox's Reformation and the scene at which in 1637 Jenny Geddes hurled a stool at a preacher trying to use Charles I's bitterly resented Anglican Prayer Book. In 1985 it was again at the centre of controversy when the dedication of the great west window to the hard drinking and womanising Robbie Burns caused outrage in the deeply moral Presbyterian community.

The High Kirk of St Giles

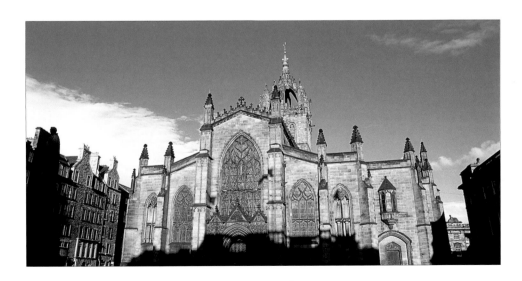

The Palace of Holyroodhouse

The Palace of Holyroodhouse marks the end of the Royal Mile. Named after the sainted Queen Margaret's holy relic of the cross, or rood, Holyrood became a royal palace in the sixteenth century. Much of Scotland's royal history took place there; favourites were murdered, Kings were married and crowned and Bonnie Prince Charlie held court in the Palace before being defeated in the '45 rebellion. King George IV caused much mirth in Edinburgh by appearing there clad in a short Royal Stewart tartan kilt and flesh coloured tights in 1822, and after Queen Victoria's visits in the nineteenth century Holyrood became the official residence of the British monarchy in Scotland.

To the north of the Old Town, and immediately identifiable on any town map due to its geometric layout, lies the elegant and spacious New Town, one of the world's most complete and unspoilt examples of Georgian architecture and town planning. Designed by the brilliant James Craig and Robert Adam, and built extraordinarily quickly between 1766 and 1840, it was one of the crowning glories of the Scottish Enlightenment. On its completion, the rich and powerful abandoned the cramped Old Town to the poor in an exodus known as the "Grand Flitting". To this day, the New Town retains an unusually large residential population for a city centre, alongside the commercial and financial institutions of Princes Street and Charlotte Square.

Edinburgh's cultural calendar is dominated by the Edinburgh Festival, the Fringe, and the Edinburgh Tattoo, all of which take place in the summer. The Festival is an unrivalled celebration of the performing and visual arts, attracting established artists from all over the globe, whereas the Fringe is informal, open to all participants, and is the testing ground for many would-be luminaries of the cultural world. While the artistic pageant is in full swing in the city below, the esplanade of the Castle explodes into life with stunning nightly displays of regimental pomp and ceremony, pipes and drums in the military and unashamedly Scottish Edinburgh Tattoo. As the Washington Post once wrote, during Festival season Edinburgh becomes "simply the best place on Earth."

To the east of Edinburgh lie the fertile lowlands of East Lothian. Bordered by the sandy beaches of the Firth of Forth to the north and the Lammermuir Hills to the south, the contrast with the industrialised areas south and west of Edinburgh is marked. The market town of Haddington was the birthplace of John Knox, whose diatribe against the French mother of Mary Queen of Scots was the inspiringly titled, "First Blast of the Trumpet against the Monstrous Regiment of Women." Close by the town of North Berwick, in which the Earl of Bothwell summoned 200 witches to cast a spell upon James VI on his return voyage from Denmark in 1590. Despite disguising himself as the Devil and indulging in some unsavoury and black practices, Bothwell's plot failed to produce the required shipwreck and the King remained very much alive. Along the coast from North Berwick stand the rugged rose pink ruins of Tantallon Castle, the mighty stronghold of the Red Douglases, which withstood three hundred years of fierce combat before succumbing to the savage onslaught of Cromwell's troops in 1651. Nearly a century later, during the last Jacobite rising in 1745, Bonnie Prince Charlie's Highlanders crushed a far superior English army at Prestonpans, inspiring him with the confidence to advance on London in the last stand for a Scottish claim to the crown.

Food in Scotland

The mystique which surrounds the traditional food of Scotland no doubt resides as much in the wonderful if somewhat obscure vocabulary involved, as in the intrinsic fascination of clootie dumplings, Selkirk bannocks, cullen skink and the like. Traditional Scottish cooking is hearty and sustaining, based on Scotland's plentiful supplies of fish and meat and supplemented with simple ingredients such as oatmeal. In fact such is the preponderance of oatmeal based foods like porridge and oatcakes that in the eighteenth century Dr Samuel Johnson was moved to include a definition of oats in his dictionary as the grain that supported the people of Scotland.

Of Scottish culinary inventions, the much maligned haggis must be the most famous. A sheep's stomach stuffed with minced offal, oatmeal and suet, haggis is the focal point of Burns' Night celebrations and is piped in with great ceremony, eulogised in Burns' "Address to the Haggis", and then stabbed open with a dirk. Traditionally preceded by cock-a-leekie soup, the haggis is accompanied by bashed neeps and chappit tatties (turnips and mashed potatoes to the uninitiated) and plenty of whisky.

The fish and shellfish, game and meat with which Scotland abounds are quite exceptional and in many cases famed worldwide. Loch Fyne oysters and kippers, smoked salmon and Arbroath Smokies (hot-smoked haddock) are outstanding, grouse is treated with an esteem that borders on the reverential and beef from native Scottish breeds such as Aberdeen Angus is considered by many to be unsurpassed in flavour. Local lamb is held in similarly high regard, the term gigot for the leg being a legacy of Scotland's Auld Alliance with France.

The Scots have traditionally had a notoriously sweet tooth and classic Scottish puddings and baking are generally of the wicked and calorific variety. Scottish shortbread and Dundee Cake are world famous whilst puddings like cranachan, based on oatmeal, are transformed from potential dreariness by the inspired, and usually liberal, addition of whisky, cream, sugar and fresh fruit. Take away the fruit and the result is the wonderfully romantic sounding Atholl Brose.

Today, Scottish-based chefs have established a new tradition which recognises Scotland's culinary heritage but which puts the bounty of fresh game, seafood, and other ingredients on their doorstep to lighter, more inventive and imaginative effect. Particularly noteworthy are the kitchens of many of the smaller country house hotels in which Scotland and her visitors delight, many of which would readily withstand comparison with the grand restaurants of Europe and the USA.

The Borders

The Scottish Borders, bounded by the Cheviot Hills to the south and the Lammermuir, Moorfoot and Pentland Hills to the North, are one of Scotland's most romantic and unspoilt regions. Empty moors, rolling hills and the incomparable Tweed Valley are strewn about with the evidence and relics of past struggles with England. The ruined abbeys and castles not only bear testament to the turbulent history of the region, but have inspired some of Scotland's best known writers; the Borders are still known as "Scott Country", such was the impact of their beauty and heritage on the prolific Sir Walter Scott.

The area was settled by the Anglo Saxons and subsequently the Anglo Normans after the Norman invasion of England in 1066. With the introduction of English style feudalism rather than the patriarchal clan system of the Highlands, the Borders became culturally separate from Celtic Scotland, engendering much of the Highland Lowland resentment and internal strife which marked Scottish history. During the eleventh century, the four great abbeys at Jedburgh, Kelso, Dryburgh and Melrose were founded by David I, probably more to establish his authority than his spirituality. They had a profound effect on the local economy and culture and, despite frequent raids by the English, survived until the Rough Wooing of the mid sixteenth century, when Henry VIII's vicious campaign led by the Earl of Hertford, and the anti-Catholic fervour of the Reformation, proved too strong a combination and all four came to a violent and fiery end.

Until the Act of Union in 1707, the Borders were a buffer between the English and the Scottish. Ravaged time and again, the cycle of sacking and rebuilding, raid and counter raid was the norm not only at the hands of the English, but also as a result of endless feuds within the great Border families and between powerful dynasties, notably the Douglases, and the Crown. The Debatable Lands in the west were in particular hotly disputed between the fourteenth and eighteenth centuries and the infamous Border Reivers raided and plundered with gusto from both sides of the border.

The gentle and mostly fertile countryside of the Borders is ideally suited to agriculture, hence sheep farming and the associated textile industries have been the mainstay of the local economy since the days of the great abbeys. During the industrial revolution knitting and weaving flourished in the Border towns, evolving into the successful knitwear and tweed industries that are now centred in Galashiels and Hawick. Tweed is particularly important in the tourist textile trade and was created by the inventive weavers of Jedburgh experimenting with two yarns. Its name is not, as would be expected, derived from the river, but from an English misprint of "tweel", a Borders word for woollen fabric.

Border scene
where strongholds watch over
the southern marches

Jedburgh Abbey

The River Tweed has marked the border with England since 1018. One of the world's most famous salmon rivers, it flows into the sea at Berwick on Tweed, which although now in England, deserves a mention for having changed hands with the Scots thirteen times between the twelfth and fifteenth centuries. "When Tweed and Powsail meet at Merlin's grave, Scotland and England shall one monarch have." Thomas Rymour made this bizarre prediction in the thirteenth century and on the day that Elizabeth I of England died in 1603, making James VI the first King of Scotland and England, the Tweed did overflow and for the first time the waters met those of Powsail Burn at the appointed spot.

Close by, in England again, is the site of the Battle of Flodden where James IV and thousands of Scots were massacred by the English in 1513 and further up the Tweed Valley are the beautiful ruins of Kelso, Melrose and Dryburgh Abbeys. Melrose is a tiny town at the foot of the three heather-covered Eildon Hills, deep within which legend has it King Arthur and his Knights sleep bound by a powerful spell. Robert the Bruce's heart was purportedly buried in the Abbey, contrary to his wishes, and in 1920 a mummified heart was discovered in the ruins. Sir Walter Scott is buried in the pink stoned ruins of Dryburgh Abbey close to his home of Abbotsford, which although fulfilling his notions of what a "romance in stone and mortar" should be, prompted Ruskin to describe as "the most incongruous pile that gentlemanly modernism ever designed."

Jedburgh, and many of the Border towns, still maintain the tradition of "The Riding of the Marches", or the Common Riding in which the boundaries of the common land are checked on horseback in recognition of less peaceful days. In Selkirk, the gathering concludes with the Casting of the Colours to commemorate the horror of Flodden, from which only one Selkirk soldier returned. Also in acknowledgement of the English is the game of Hand Ba' played every February in Jedburgh. Not a game for the fainthearted, a small leather ball, originally the head of an Englishman, is wrested from one end of the town to the other by all male teams from above the Market Place, the Uppies, or below it, the Downies.

Sport in Scotland

Curling, 'Scotland's ain game' and effectively bowls on ice played with large flattened spheres of stone, reflects the harsh winter conditions prevalent over much of Scotland. Both Scotland and the Low Countries have laid claims to be the originator of the sport: however, the wealth of curling stones or 'granites' unearthed in diggings and retrieved from lochs over the centuries, and the lack of such finds from Holland, lend far greater credibility to Scotland's claim. Certainly Holland has no relic to match the 'Stirling Stone', Scotland earliest curling relic dated 1511 now held in the Smith Institute in Stirling. The Royal Caledonian Curling Club was formed in 1838 to regularise the rules of the game, and together with overseas tours by Scots was the guiding force behind the spread of the game to ice-bound countries throughout the world. The Royal Club's 'Grand Match' between the north and south of Scotland contested on a frozen loch by upwards of 2,500 curlers, remains one of the country's most spectacular sporting occasions.

The two principal British codes of football, rugby and soccer, are something of a national obsession in Scotland, and were exported from this northern base to the far corners of the world during the days of British imperial power. While English administrators were introducing the languid skills of cricket to fast-learning natives, Scottish engineers and settling farmers carried with them the joys of their more physical pastimes. It is intriguing to reflect that the past, present, and no doubt future world rugby dominance of New Zealand - "Scotland in the antipodes" - is the direct legacy of that stern breed who actually built the Empire. Rugby in Scotland is especially vibrant in the Borders and Lowlands, and the majestic national stadium at Murrayfield in Edinburgh resonates with patriotic fervour on international days, when large men in sheepskin coats from around the world congregate in the capital city, and the proud wearers of the blue jersey uphold a long tradition of consistently performing well beyond the natural expectations of a country of Scotland's size.

In 'fitba' also Scotland continues to punch above her weight on the world stage. Opportunities to humiliate England, the Auld Enemy, have been limited since the demise of the annual fixture (after Scottish supporters attempted to carry the English national stadium home in triumph) but the national team has a record of qualification for the World Cup, and the team's supporters a well-earned reputation abroad for good humour in victory or defeat, that are the envy of their southern rivals. Domestically, the powers in the game are concentrated in the cities; Edinburgh, Dundee, Aberdeen, and especially Glasgow, where the sporting rivalry between Celtic and Rangers is given an added tang by centuries-old religious differences. A final and fascinating modern counterpart to Scotland's historic role in exporting the world's most popular sport has been the recent dominance over English football enjoyed by Scotsmen, begun by Sir Matt Busby in the sixties through Bill Shankly and Bob Paisley in the seventies and eighties, to Kenny Dalglish and Alex Ferguson in the nineties.

The South West

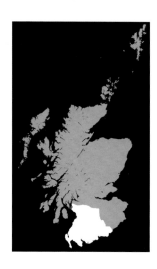

It has been said that the south western corner of Scotland, stretching from the Solway Firth to the western end of the Firth of Clyde, is a miniature version of the country as a whole. The Solway coast leading away from Dumfries is breathtaking, as are the lonely mountains, forests and moors of Galloway. Ayrshire's rich agricultural land and rolling hills are gentler, although the landscape becomes increasingly industrialised towards Glasgow. Unspoilt by commercial pressures, the South West has an atmosphere of peace and tranquillity enhanced by its great tracts of natural beauty and the benign influence of the Gulf Stream which endows it with the gentlest of Scottish climates.

Soon after the Romans left Britain, Galloway, as the South West was known, was settled by Celtic Britons whose clan Chieftains were not only unruly but fiercely independent and whose allegiance lay with the Vikings rather than the Scots. Insurrection was rife and it was not until the thirteenth century that Galloway was to any degree integrated into Scotland. Robert the Bruce's campaign for Scottish independence was launched there in the early fourteenth century and although the wars with England ravaged much of the South West, nationalism and a common enemy proved a great unifying force. Galloway was henceforward firmly part of Scotland, even if the powerful nobility continued to rebel against the monarchy.

As in the Borders, the bleak fortresses and ruins scattered throughout bear witness to the brutality of much of its history. Not only did the English repeatedly attack towns, abbeys and strongholds, but the Reformation was valiantly supported in the South West and some of the worst atrocities were perpetrated by Scots in the name of Presbyterianism and religious zeal.

Dumfries was a prime target for the English in the fifteenth and sixteenth centuries. A thriving seaport and trading centre, its affluence was an irresistible magnet for invading forces and the town was devastated on numerous occasions,

The Solway
where sea meets sky
in a vaste and lonely embrace

as a result of which the oldest building is seventeenth century, even though Dumfries existed in Roman times. Perhaps the greatest claims to fame Dumfries has are due to Robert the Bruce and Robert Burns. In 1306 Robert the Bruce stabbed to death his rival to the Scottish throne in the Greyfriars Kirk, thereby indirectly ending the Wars of Independence and bestowing on Scotland a steady line of succession through his Stewart descendants. Nearly five hundred years later, Robert Burns died in the town and despite being buried in a simple grave on his death in 1796, was moved to better things in a purpose-built Neoclassical mausoleum twenty years later.

Sweetheart Abbey

South of Dumfries, the triangular Caerlaverock Castle is one of Scotland's finest and most unusual mediaeval castles. Set on a beautiful stretch of coast, it was besieged by Edward I in search of Robert the Bruce, who later recaptured and dismantled it to thwart the English. It was rebuilt at the end of the sixteenth century and just six years after the outstanding Renaissance apartments were added, attacked by the Covenanters. The Earl of Nithsdale surrendered after a siege of four months and his newly completed castle was utterly destroyed.

Close by are the ruins of Sweetheart Abbey, so called for its patron, the lovesick Devorguilla de Balliol, who carried her husband's heart in an ivory box with her for sixteen years before she died. The opulence of the building was extraordinary for the thirteenth century and a clear reflection of the wealth the diligent monks had accumulated from draining the marshes and converting them into productive farmland.

In stark contrast to the romance of Sweetheart Abbey is the forbidding ruin of Threave Castle, the seat and home of the notorious Black Douglases. James Douglas, founder of the family fortunes, had made his mark fighting with Robert the Bruce and his son was created Lord of Galloway and Warden of the Marches. An Earldom in 1358 and several good marriages to secure vast landownings made the Black Douglases a fearsome dynasty, who not only terrorised the English, but whose immense power and ambition were the bane of several Stuart Kings.

To the west, on a remote promontory jutting into the Irish Sea is the tiny village of Whithorn, in which a small white chapel, "Candida Casa", was built in 397AD by St Ninian. The size of the chapel belied the immeasurable impact it had on Scotland, for it was the first Christian Church north of Hadrian's Wall and became the centre from which Christian missionaries set out to convert the pagan Britons and Picts. St Ninian's shrine was a popular pilgrimage destination until the end of the sixteenth century when such popish customs were banned under the austere influence of the Reformation.

Due north of Whithorn in the Ayrshire village of Alloway, Robert Burns was born on January 25th, 1759. The unwitting cause of many a party to celebrate his birthday on Burns' Night, the world famous "farmer poet" was a pivotal literary figure in the Scottish Enlightenment and did much to restore Scottish pride after Union with England and the concomitant loss of Scottish identity.

Robert Burns

Robert Burns, the "ploughman poet", was born in Ayrshire in 1759. The son of an unsuccessful farmer, his impoverished and strictly Calvinistic childhood had a profound influence on his writing and views. His father's death in penury following financial pressure from unsympathetic landlords endowed Burns with a lasting dislike of the upper classes, which manifested itself in several of his wryly satirical poems. His mother was illiterate and he was largely self taught, establishing at an early age a love of poetry and Scottish folk songs that was to form the basis of his literary success.

The combination of his father's death, his own inability to earn a living from farming and the threatening father of his mistress Jean Armour prompted Burns to write an anthology of poems in order to raise enough money to emigrate to Jamaica. "Poems, Chiefly in the Scottish Dialect" won him immediate acclaim and in 1787 he moved to Edinburgh, the hub of the Scottish literary Enlightenment, where he was lionised by the establishment of which he so disapproved. Unmoved by his new found status, which coincidentally did little to relieve his financial situation, he became known as a rustic genius, an image he made little effort to dispel, appreciating the licence such a reputation bestowed on his somewhat relaxed moral standards and fondness for the good life.

Two years and several liaisons later, the lasting benefits of which were some passionate love poems, Burns finally married Jean Armour and became an Excise Officer to supplement his income. After another failed attempt at farming, the family moved to Dumfries where, aged thirty seven, Burns died of rheumatic fever.

Burns' reputation as a man of the people and the fact that he wrote in Lallans, a Scottish Lowland dialect, when the fashion was towards all things English were major factors in his success. His poetry and songs concentrated on homely themes, the emphasis lying on human nature in its shortcomings as well as its virtues. His humour and irreverence, particularly with regard to the hypocrisy of the landed classes and the Kirk, won him widespread popularity whilst his romantic nationalism after Union with England did much to restore Scottish pride and confidence.

Burns' Night, his birthday, is celebrated the world over with haggis, whisky and bagpipes on January 25th and concludes with one of his best known works, "Auld Lang Syne." The tradition is unwaveringly upheld to ensure that Burns' memory is feted in the style befitting to a Scottish hero.

Glasgow and the Clyde

Glasgow is Scotland's largest city, a vibrant cultural mecca that has undergone a transformation of extraordinary proportions in recent years. During the nineteenth and early twentieth century Glasgow's wealth and industrial prominence were such that it was known as "the second city of the Empire." The nadir to which it subsequently plunged was thus in cruel contrast to the glory of bygone times, and it is from this low point that Glasgow has reinvented itself to be voted City of Culture in 1990 and City of Architecture and Design in 1999.

Glasgow was first put on the map by St Ninian, who gave the site his blessing in 397AD. St Mungo, patron saint of Glasgow, was subsequently buried there and in 1136 the cathedral was built over his grave. Glasgow University was founded in the fifteenth century and, until the Old College was built, based in the sacristy of the cathedral, which itself became remarkable by omission during the following century for being the only mainland mediaeval cathedral to escape destruction at the hands of the Reformers.

In 1674, the first cargo of tobacco arrived in Glasgow from Virginia. After the Treaty of Union with England, which removed many of the restrictions on Scotland's trading activities, trade with America boomed and by the mid-eighteenth century Glasgow had become the most important tobacco port in Britain. However, the American War of Independence destroyed Britain's virtual monopoly over American tobacco exports and the industry collapsed, to be replaced by a burgeoning cotton industry.

With the invention of James Watt's steam engine and the installation of the first mechanised looms at Paisley in 1792, the pace of the industrial revolution gathered momentum. Under Watt's supervision, nineteen miles of the Clyde were deepened enabling ships to reach the docks of Glasgow, as a result of which industrialisation, fuelled by coal from the nearby Lanarkshire coalfields, spread

Ingram Street

rapidly through the city and surrounding areas. When the cotton industry declined in the 1860s, the emphasis shifted to heavy industry and shipbuilding and by the beginning of the twentieth century, Glasgow and the Clyde area were making "one fifth of the steel, one third of the shipping tonnage, one half of the marine engine horsepower, one third of the railway locomotives and rolling stock and most of the sewing machines in the United Kingdom."

Glasgow
al fresco dining
at the Italian Centre

Meanwhile, cheap labour requirements, the Highland Clearances and the Irish potato famine had provoked a huge influx of workers to the region. The population of Glasgow leapt from 17,000 in 1740 to nearly 800,000 at the end of the nineteenth century, and the resulting overcrowding and appalling living conditions had desperate consequences for the working classes. In the latter half of the nineteenth century life expectancy was no more than thirty years, disease and alcoholism were rife and the Gorbals became known as the worst slums in Europe.

Nonetheless vast fortunes had been made by the "tobacco lords", shipping magnates and industrial barons and with this wealth Glasgow and the Clyde were transformed during Victorian times by grand and confident architectural schemes. After the first World War, economic decline and in particular the death of the shipbuilding industry devastated the industrial base of the region, creating widespread unemployment and a malaise from which Glasgow has only recently recovered.

Architecturally Glasgow is predominantly Victorian, although the elegant and gracious Merchant City to the east of George Square dates from the eighteenth century. Built by the wealthy tobacco lords, it was a planned development of warehouses and homes similar in principle to Edinburgh's New Town. With the coming of the Victorians, and more specifically the wherewithal to commission the best architects and build accordingly, came the magnificence that characterises much of central Glasgow today. West of George Square is the Victorian commercial centre, which so impressed John Betjeman that he was moved to describe it as "the greatest Victorian city in the world."

At the end of the nineteenth century, Charles Rennie Mackintosh rose to fame almost overnight when, aged twenty eight, his plans for the Glasgow School of Art were published. One of the most innovative architects and designers of the time, he evolved Art Nouveau Glasgow style, and although his influence was greater in Europe than in Britain, some of his best and most striking work is in his home town.

To the west of Glasgow lies Greenock, birth place of James Watt, whose brilliance as an engineer led to the invention of an efficient steam engine, one of the great catalysts of the industrial revolution. To the south east, it was from the Clyde Valley village of Blantyre that the great Victorian missionary explorer, David Livingstone embarked on his extraordinary career. A mill worker at the age of ten, he educated himself at night, took a medical degree and set off to explore Africa, dying in 1873 in his quest to find the source of the Nile.

Further up the valley are Lanark and New Lanark, the former the site of William Wallace's famous scuffle with the law which sparked the Wars of Independence and the latter a landmark in social and industrial history. David Dale founded the village in 1785, having seen the potential of harnessing the power of the Clyde to his cotton weaving machinery while his son in law, Robert Owen, was a committed social reformer who believed passionately in nurturing the workforce to maximise their potential and ultimately benefit the company. His model village included, along with schools and a co-operative store, the world's first day care nursery, an unheard of provision at the time and a rarity even now.

Argyll

Argyll (the name derives from the Gaelic for "Boundary of the Gaels") is remote and beautiful, sparsely populated and wonderfully varied in its scenery. The coast is indented by long glacial inlets and sea lochs penetrating deep into the heart of the region and whilst the south is typically Lowland, warmed by the influence of the Gulf Stream, the islands and north of the region are bleaker and more akin to the Highlands in appearance.

During the third and fourth centuries, the Irish Celts settled in Argyll, calling it Dalriada, and by 500 AD, a stronghold had been built at Dunadd, from which the Irish, confusingly called the "Scotti" by the Romans, eventually conquered the whole of Scotland. After a brief spell of Nordic domination, Somerled, King of Argyll, held sway until ousted by the MacDonalds, who were in turn supplanted by the Campbells, Dukes of Argyll and even now the largest landowners in the region.

In the eighteenth century the third Duke of Argyll built the classic planned town of Inverary at the top of Loch Fyne to distance the townspeople from his residence. Set in idyllic surroundings, Inverary is a model of Georgian elegance and architectural restraint, qualities conspicuously lacking in the striking if somewhat eccentric neo-Gothic, neo-Baronial Castle he built at the same time and which is still the seat of Clan Campbell.

To the south, the beautiful peninsula of Kintyre is separated from the mainland by the narrowest of land bridges. As a result of this happy geographic circumstance Kintyre became part of the Hebridean Kingdom of the Norsemen in the eleventh century when Magnus Barelegs, who had been proffered any island he could circumnavigate by Malcolm III, carried his Viking longship over the strand.

Of the islands of Argyll, which include those west of Kintyre and the southern islands of the Inner Hebrides, only Mull has made a significant recovery from the devastation wrought on their populations by the Highland Clearances. This beautiful island, in which great tracts of moorland surround mountainous peaks,

Iona

is home to the picturesque port of Tobermory and the village of Calgary, where Colonel McLeod set sail for the New World and after which he named the fort he founded in Alberta, Canada. Mull is also the stepping stone to the tiny island of Iona, where St Columba established the Celtic Church in the sixth century and from where he set out to convert the pagans of Scotland and Northern England. Despite Iona's turbulent history - it was violently desecrated by first the Vikings and then the Reformers - the island is imbued with a profound sense of holiness, as befits "the cradle of Christianity" in Scotland.

Wildlife

There are few regions of Scotland's size which can boast its array of glorious wildlife. The magnificent native red deer, immortalised in Landseer's painting "The Monarch of the Glen", is probably Scotland's most famous beast, as well as one of its most problematic. Since the eradication of the wolf in the seventeenth century, red deer numbers have spiralled and now pose a major threat to Scotland's woodland. Reindeer, extinct in Scotland since the twelfth century, have recently been reintroduced to the Cairngorms.

Cattle, once the currency of Highland life and the frequent cause of raid and counter-raid between clans, were mainly supplanted by sheep during the Highland Clearances; however, benign-looking but ill-tempered Highland Cattle still roam wild in the Highlands and Islands. Feral mink, escapees from mink farms, are becoming more common, otters are to be found in fresh and salt water locations, while wild cats and pine martens hide in the moors and forests. To adapt to the harsh conditions of upland Scottish winters mountain hares and stoats assume a camouflage of white fur, that of the stoat being the ermine which for centuries has adorned the robes of nobility.

Scotland's fresh waters are renowned for their salmon, sea trout and brown trout. Most of the great salmon rivers lie on the east coast and are fished for salmon returning to spawn at the precise location from which they left for the sea years beforehand, whilst the hill lochs and streams teem with shy and nervous brown trout. The rich waters of the surrounding seas make Scotland an internationally important haven for seabirds, with cliffs on the mainland and islands sustaining raucous multitudes of gannets, auks and gulls during the breeding season.

The red grouse is Scotland's most highly prized game bird. Grouse represent a significant income for Scottish estates and the young heather on which they thrive is aggressively generated by burning great swathes of moorland. The tiny ptarmigan, or white grouse, live above the snow line and continue to flourish in the Cairngorms, camouflaged against the mottled landscape in summer and moulting to pure white in winter. The turkey-like capercaillie - its name derives from the Gaelic for "bird of the woodlands" - is the largest of the grouse family. Encouraged by recent commercial plantings and careful management, populations cling on deep amid the great coniferous forests.

For millennia Scotland has been a haven for massive numbers of birds escaping the Arctic winter. Every autumn wildfowl and waders in their hundreds of thousands fly in from as far afield as Siberia, while more solitary visitors are the snowy owls and gyrfalcons which intermittently winter on Scotland's northern extremes, the former on rare occasions staying on to breed in the spring. Throughout the year Scotland is home to many magnificent birds of prey: peregrines and merlins on seacliff and moor, goshawks once more patrolling their ancestral haunts in the dark caledonian forests, and of course the majestic golden eagle, living symbol of the grandeur of the Highlands. Ospreys, absent for decades, now nest regularly at Loch Garten near the Spey.

Stirling and the Central Lowlands

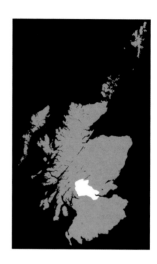

The city of Stirling lies astride the River Forth in the Central Lowlands, which themselves lie at the very heart of Scotland. Near the head of the Firth of Forth, Stirling is surrounded by the magical glens and forests of the Trossachs to the west, the rolling Campsies to the south, and to the northeast the Ochil Hills. Running diagonally just to the north of Stirling, the great geological Highland Fault Line physically cleaves the gentle Lowlands from the wild and rugged Highlands. In short, it is an area not only of great natural beauty, but one which has been of enormous historical significance due to its incomparable and commanding geographical position.

Stirling was once described as the key to Scotland and the most important strategic location in the country. Not only was it the main bridging point over the Forth, but the marshy and treacherous wetlands of the Carse of Forth were only passable from the town; whoever controlled Stirling effectively controlled the gateway between north and south. It is thus hardly surprising that the name of Stirling originated in the phrase "place of striving" and that the castle, built on a volcanic plug and therefore a formidable vantage point, changed hands in the course of Scottish history more often than any other Scottish stronghold.

During the Wars of Independence, Stirling's strategic importance was not lost on the English and the town was witness to two of the most significant battles in Scottish history. In 1297 William Wallace routed a far superior English army at Stirling Bridge, and in a victory that was to signify the turning point in Scotland's struggle for independence, Robert the Bruce crushingly defeated the English at nearby Bannockburn in 1314.

A favoured residence of the Stuart kings, both the town and castle of Stirling flourished between the fifteenth and seventeenth centuries, the odd fragment of unsavoury history notwithstanding. In 1452 the insubordinate and overpowerful

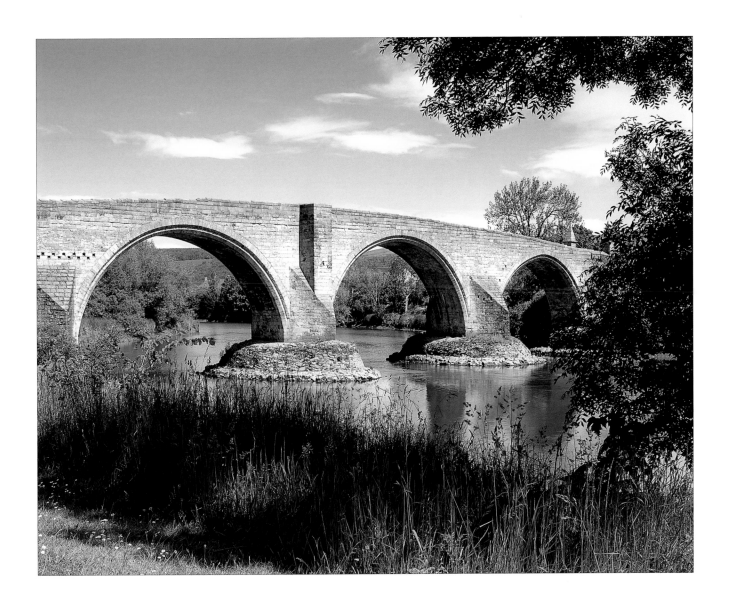

The Old Bridge at Stirling
strategic key to Scotland

Earl of Douglas was invited to dinner by James II and brutally murdered, whereupon his body, or what was left of it, was flung unceremoniously from a castle window. James II, III and V were born at Stirling and it was to the safety of the palace that in 1528 James V escaped from the Douglases dressed as a commoner, an event commemorated in one of the many Renaissance carvings which adorn the castle. Mary Queen of Scots was crowned there at only one week old and as an indirect result Stirling acquired its magnificent town walls. Built as protection against the mid sixteenth century Rough Wooing, Henry VIII's less than subtle attempt to gain Mary's hand in marriage for his son, they are the most complete surviving town walls in Scotland today.

To the west of Stirling on the edge of the Central Lowlands is the glorious Loch Lomond, Britain's largest inland waterway. In the early days of Scottish history, the loch lay at the meeting point of the Kingdoms of Dalriada, Strathclyde and Pictland. Given the volatility of the warring tribes, it was perhaps unsurprising that the thirty odd islands in the loch were frequently used by Christian missionaries beating a hasty retreat from the pagan and savage Celts. Framed dramatically by hills and woodland on its "bonnie bonnie banks", the loch is known the world over from the sad lament reputedly written by one of Bonnie Prince Charlie's followers on the eve of his execution, which even now provokes a melancholy yearning in Scots abroad for their homeland.

Loch Lomond

The fairytale Trossachs to the east of Loch Lomond include some of the most wonderful and varied scenery in Scotland. They were home to Rob Roy, the seventeenth century outlaw, whose fall from grace and subsequent life of violence was much romanticised by Sir Walter Scott. Rob Roy was leader of the wild Clan Gregor whose dubious activities and extortion rackets involving the levying of black meal led to the coining of the term 'blackmail'.

In stark contrast to the tranquillity of the rural hills and lochs are the industrialised landscapes of the Forth Valley. Transport links with Glasgow via the eighteenth century Forth Clyde Canal and later with Edinburgh via the Union Canal had an immeasurable impact on the region, which was transformed unrecognisably during the industrial revolution. By 1800 the Carron Ironworks at Falkirk were Europe's largest producer of artillery, making amongst other things "carronades", or small cannons, for Nelson's fleet. Falkirk also had more immediate military connections in that it was the site of William Wallace's final defeat at English hands in 1298 and of one of Bonnie Prince Charlie's last victories over the Hanoverians as he retreated northwards after the '45 Jacobite rebellion.

Relics of an earlier conflict, the Roman invasion of Scotland, lie just to the west of Falkirk. Twenty years after Hadrian's Wall was built from Solway to Tyne, an optimistic attempt to push the Roman border northwards resulted in the Antonine Wall, stretching across the waist of Scotland from the Forth to the Clyde. It was a shortlived venture, lasting a mere forty years before the Romans abandoned their posts and retreated to south of Hadrian's Wall, but one which left such fascinating monuments as Rough Castle, a fort built in 142 AD to defend the wall against the bellicose northerners.

The Trossachs
Loch Achray and Loch Venacher
from the slopes of Ben Venue

Tartan and the clans

The roots of the Highland clans lie in the ancient Kingdoms of the north and west of Scotland where the Irish and the Norsemen held sway in the earliest days of Scottish history. Clan society was based on the concept of a common ancestry which bound the "children" of the clan together in an unwritten but unassailable patriarchal system, "Mac" denoting son of, hence for example Clan MacDonald. The father figure of the Clan Chief commanded total power over his clansmen, whose sense of belonging was absolute and whose loyalty was amply rewarded by the care of a society based on the Celtic principles of kindness, duty and devotion.

Clan lands belonged to the Chief, who let them via the clan hierarchy to the tacksmen, his closest kin, who sublet to the tenants. Below the tenants came the landless crofters who were given the right to basic subsistence farming on a small strip of land. Rents were often paid in the form of military service and the clan, essentially a military unit, operated on a system of trust and goodwill. This is not to say that clan life was peaceful. The Clan Chiefs operated as virtually autonomous monarchs, paying scant heed to the political powers of the day, and feuding between rival clans and the crown was almost constant. As one observer wrote, "They spend all their time in wars and, when there is no war, they fight one another."

After the Jacobite Rising of 1745 the clan system was vigorously suppressed by the English and the traditional Highland way of life faded into oblivion, a process accelerated by the Highland Clearances.

Nonetheless the clan spirit did survive, the famous names live on, and Clan Chiefs are officially recognised to this day.

During the seventeenth century tartan was adopted to express membership of a clan, the first records being of specific designs worn by the Hebridean islanders and preserved on "sett" sticks. Shortly afterwards the Campbells claimed a tartan for themselves, so initiating the tradition of a clan and its members having exclusive rights to a particular pattern.

Tartan was traditionally worn in the form of a long single piece of cloth wound around the waist and passed over the shoulder, from which evolved the kilt and full regalia of Highland Dress. Spun from local wool and coloured with plant dyes, the original plaids were not only hardwearing and virtually showerproof, but their broken pattern was excellent camouflage.

Tartan was adopted by the Lowlanders at the beginning of the eighteenth century as a sign of support for the Jacobite Rebellions, after which it was banned between 1746 and 1782 as part of the Government's measures to subjugate the clans. It was not until the nineteenth century when George IV appeared in Edinburgh clad in Royal Stewart tartan and Sir Walter Scott's kilted Highlanders fired the nation's imagination that tartan underwent one renaissance, and then another when Queen Victoria bought Balmoral and swathed both it and her employees in tartan and the Balmoral Estate tweed designed by Prince Albert.

The Kingdom of Fife

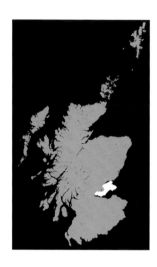

The ancient Kingdom of Fife was christened by the Picts in the fourth century and lies to the north of Edinburgh on a peninsula bounded by the waters of the Tay, the North Sea and the Firth of Forth. It is a unique part of Scotland, fiercely maintaining its own identity and integrity, and one in which, despite its diminutive size, much that shaped Scottish history took place.

Fife is a scant fifty miles across at widest, but nonetheless there are distinct differences in the landscape within it. The south is semi-industrial, the north predominantly rural and in the centre lie the Lomond Hills and the rich agricultural land of the Howe of Fife. Rugged windswept cliffs and silver beaches make up the coastline, along which are dotted picturesque fishing villages, many reminiscent architecturally of the trade which flourished from the Middle Ages with the Low Countries and the Baltic.

In southern Fife, Culross is one of the best preserved and prettiest towns in Scotland. Established in the fifth century, it became a religious centre in the sixth after the birth of St Mungo, later patron saint of Glasgow. George Bruce, a descendant of Robert the Bruce, was largely responsible for transforming the fortunes of Culross at the turn of the sixteenth century by mining for coal in undersea tunnels and nurturing trading links with Holland, the influence of which is still clearly visible in the gabled houses of the town.

Dunfermline, historic capital of Scotland, lies just inland and was once the world centre of the damask linen trade. It was here that Malcolm III offered refuge to his future wife, Margaret, shipwrecked whilst fleeing the Norman invasion of England, whose reforms of the Celtic Church and anglicising influence had an immeasurable impact on the course of Scottish history. Six Scottish monarchs are buried in the Abbey, and the town was the birthplace of Charles I, the last Scottish King to be born on Scottish soil. Andrew Carnegie was also born in Dunfermline, the son of

a poor weaver. He became one of the world's richest industrialists and philanthropists, opening the first of his free libraries in Dunfermline in 1881 and, in an act of somewhat dubious motivation, buying and donating Pittencrief Park, from which he had been banned by the Laird, to the town in 1902. He had a great passion for his home town, writing, "The child who is granted the opportunity to grow up in an area like Dunfermline draws in with every breath poetry and romance ... These first impressions ... touch his soul, they fan the spark within into a flame, they make something different, something greater out of him, than would have been the case if he had been less fortunate in the place where he was born."

Crail
typical village
of the Fife coast

St Andrews University
*red-robed students on their
traditional Sunday pier walk*

Further along the south coast on a dark night in 1286, a horse carrying Alexander III stumbled and fell from the cliffs at Kinghorn, taking the King to his death and thereby not only ending the reign of the Celtic monarchs but leading directly to the Wars of Independence between England and Scotland. Of the resulting Stuart dynasty, James II built one of the first fortresses specifically adapted for artillery warfare in the latter half of the fifteenth century at Kirkcaldy. James was fanatical about firearms, although in one of history's great ironies he was killed by an exploding Scottish cannon, and Ravenscraig Castle was not only imposing but virtually impregnable, designed as it was both to withstand and deliver cannon fire.

Towards the centre of Fife, the splendid Palace of Falkland was the country residence of the Stuarts for several hundred years and was originally confiscated by James I in his campaign to reassert Crown authority over the powerful and dissident nobles at the beginning of the fifteenth century. Rebuilt by James IV and V, the influence of the latter's two French wives is easily identified in some of the Palace's architectural similarities to the Châteaux of the Loire Valley. Still owned by the Crown, Falkland's royal, or real, tennis courts are the oldest of their kind in Britain; they were built for James V in 1539 and are in use even now.

North of the pretty old fashioned fishing villages of the East Neuk is the world famous town of St Andrews. Legend has it that in the fourth century the Greek monk, St Regulus, dreamt that he should take the relics of St Andrew from the Island of Patras to the edge of the western world and build a city there. Shipwrecked off Fife, he built a shrine on the site of the cathedral, St Andrew became Scotland's patron saint and the town evolved into the religious centre of the country by the fifteenth century. In 1546 George Wishart, one of John Knox's fellow Reformers, was burnt at the stake in front of St Andrew's Castle, ostensibly for plotting the murder of Cardinal Beaton, on whose head, or the severance thereof, lay an English booty of £1000. Beaton was duly murdered in the castle and Knox, whose principles extended to approving of murder for the right reasons, was one of the group of Protestants which subsequently occupied the castle for a year, building meanwhile what are thought to be the finest siege tunnels in Europe.

In tandem with its historical significance, St Andrews has two other outstanding features. The University, established in 1410, is the oldest in Scotland but there is little doubt that St Andrews' true claim to fame lies in its much vaunted golfing traditions and institutions. The Royal and Ancient Golf Club, the sixteenth century Old Course and the fact that the British Open has been held there on rotation since 1873 are but a few of the reasons that St Andrews is regarded as the spiritual centre of the golfing world.

Golf

Legend has it that golf was invented centuries ago by a Scottish shepherd casually swinging his stick to hit stones into rabbit holes; that the game originated in Scotland is rarely disputed, although the whereabouts of the great occurrence is frequently a subject of heated debate. Gaelic for hit, "gowf" had become such an obsession in Scotland by 1457 that James II was prompted to ban it for interfering with the army's archery practice. "Gowf and fitba...not to be usit" were his words in the first written record of the game, a sentiment no doubt oft repeated by golfing widows the world over.

Golf was a favoured pastime of the Scottish monarchs, including Mary Queen of Scots, and was popularised in England only after James VI succeeded to the English throne. William IV's patronage of the Society of St Andrews Golfers elevated its status to the exclusive Royal and Ancient Golf Club in 1834, recognised since the end of the nineteenth century as golf's international ruling body. Ancient though it is, the St Andrews Club was formed in 1754, ten years after the Gentleman Golfers of Leith, which lays claim to being the oldest golf club in the world, and from which emanated some of the earliest rules of the game.

There are over four hundred golf courses in Scotland, more per capita than anywhere else in the world. The links courses arrayed along the spectacular coastline are justifiably famous whilst many inland courses are of a similarly excellent standard; St Andrews, Muirfield, Turnberry and Gleneagles are but a few of the legendary names that render Scotland a golfing paradise and the focus of the golfing world.

Perth, Dundee and the Surroundings

Heather covered glens, tranquil lochs and bleak moors framed by the magnificent Grampian mountains render Perthshire and Angus two of the most beautiful counties in Scotland. The "silvery Tay", to quote the memorably awful poet William McGonagall, runs majestically from Loch Tay in western Perthshire through wide wooded valleys to the Firth of Tay, from which the coastline curves north in a series of dramatic red sandstone cliffs and sandy beaches. Between Perth and Dundee lie the rich and fertile lands of the Carse of Gowrie and throughout the entire region are littered the relics of the mysterious Pictish civilisation which held sway in north east Scotland until the ninth century.

Lying on the banks of the Tay, Perth became the capital of Scotland in the twelfth century due to its proximity to Scone, coronation place of the Scottish Kings. In 990 AD, legend has it that Scotland acquired the thistle as a national emblem after an invading Danish force attempted to ambush King Kenneth II's army at night just west of the town. Stealth was paramount, shoes was banned and the humble thistle saved the day by provoking howls of anguish from the unsuspecting and injured Danes. James I, whose intelligent and well meaning reforms failed to endear him to all his subjects, was assassinated in the Priory in 1437, and in 1559 the Presbyterian Reformer John Knox so inflamed his congregation with his galvinising rhetoric that "the rascal multitude" went on an iconoclastic rampage, destroying all four of Perth's monasteries and sparking an explosion in the pace of the Reformation. Historical damage notwithstanding, Sir Walter Scott wrote, "Perth, so eminent for the beauty of its situation, is a place of great antiquity." It is still a charming market town and home to the sales of Aberdeen Angus cattle, famed the world over.

Scone Palace, just north of Perth, was built in the grounds of the Abbey destroyed by Knox's religious vandals in 1559. In the sixth century, the coronation Stone of Destiny, often called the Stone of Scone, was brought to the west coast kingdom

of Dalriada from Ireland, whence the Celtic "Scots" of Dalriada originated. In the ninth century King Kenneth MacAlpin took the stone to Scone having conquered the Picts, where it remained until 1296 when Edward I removed it during the Wars of Independence to London. In 1950 a group of daring Nationalists abducted the stone from Westminster Abbey to Arbroath, and it has now been officially returned to Edinburgh Castle, with due pomp and ceremony, and with the blessing of the Prime Minister.

Perth
ancient capital on the Tay

Aberfeldy Bridge
designed by William Adam
by order of General Wade

North of Perth in the Tay valley, the pretty town of Dunkeld was the religious centre of Kenneth MacAlpin's partially united Kingdom of Scotland in the ninth century and home to St Columba's relics, transported there from Iona in the extraordinary Monymusk Reliquary. The Cathedral is one of Scotland's most elegant and idyllically situated ruins despite being damaged in the Reformation and burnt during the Jacobite resistance to the Dutch William of Orange. Close by across Thomas Telford's seven arched bridge over the Tay lies the tiny village Birnam and what remains of Birnam Wood. "I will not be afraid of death and bane, Till Birnam Forest come to Dunsinane," were Shakespeare's words on the subject of Macbeth's immortality, or lack of it.

The first skirmish of the 1689 Jacobite rebellion which resulted in the sacking of Dunkeld took place close by in the beautiful and rugged gorge of Killiecrankie, where the Highlanders loyal to the Stuart James VII were led by Graham of Claverhouse to a rousing victory over the English troops. Later Jacobite risings forced the English to build a network of military roads and bridges to open up the troublesome Highlands under the aegis of General Wade. The road through Pitlochry was one of the first, built at the beginning of the eighteenth century, and the wonderfully elegant bridge at Aberfeldy, designed by the Palladian William Adam, conclusively proved that practicality and beauty are not mutually exclusive.

On the wooded slopes above the River Garry stands the whimsical white Blair Castle. The seat of the Duke of Atholl, the castle was the last in Britain to be besieged as a result of split loyalties between the incumbent Duke and his younger brother who led the Jacobite Army in the fading days of the '45 rebellion. Queen Victoria was a guest in the 1840s, and it was then that she granted the Duke of Atholl the unique privilege of maintaining his own private army, the Atholl Highlanders, who still meet and parade on the last Sunday in May every year.

To the west of Blair Atholl rises Schiehallion, one of Scotland's loveliest mountains. The name means "The Fairy Hill of the Caledonians" and its almost flawless conical shape lends it well to the local nickname "The Maiden's Breast." It was used in 1774 by the Revd Dr Maskelyne in his calculations of the earth's mass, which, given the basic instruments available at the time proved remarkably accurate. On the other side of Loch Tummel, the Queen's View is a breathtaking vantage point over a panorama of majestic scenery, including the perfect peak of Schiehallion. Queen Victoria had a somewhat unsuccessful picnic there in 1844, but the spot was apparently named before her visit, probably after Mary Queen of Scots, who used to hunt from Atholl.

In a magnificent position on the Tay estuary, Dundee has been the scene of many a conflict throughout Scottish history. Captured by Edward I, besieged by Henry VIII and destroyed by Cromwell in the seventeenth century, it is little wonder that there are few buildings of any great antiquity in the town. Trading links with Flanders and the Baltic were the stimulus for Dundee's original development and by the nineteenth century Dundee was one of Scotland's most prominent commercial centres. Captain Scott's ship the Discovery was built there for his polar expeditions in 1900 and now lies on the waterfront, as does HMS Unicorn, the oldest British warship still afloat, built in 1824.

Glamis Castle

North of Dundee, Glamis Castle must be every child's vision of what a Scottish castle should look like. Turrets, battlements and a spectacular mountain backdrop combine to make Glamis, the fictional setting of Macbeth's exploits and reputedly the most haunted castle in Scotland, the most romantic and archetypal of castles. It has remained in the Lyon family by direct descent since the fourteenth century and was the childhood home of Queen Elizabeth, the Queen Mother.

On the peaceful Angus coast, lies the twelfth century fishing port of Arbroath. Famous not only for its renowned smokies, in 1320 the inspirational Declaration of Arbroath was signed at the Abbey by a group of Scottish nobles in one of the greatest affirmations of national intent ever crafted. In it, Scotland repudiated English sovereignty and declared her independence from England and Rome with the words;

"We fight not for glory, nor riches, nor honour, but only for that liberty which no true man relinquishes but with his life."

Loch Rannoch and Schiehallion

Field sports

For the lucky few, the mention of Scotland conjures up wonderful images of grouse shooting on heather clad moors, stalking over deserted hills and fishing the magnificent salmon rivers of the east coast. Scotland is a sporting paradise in which unrivalled hunting, shooting and fishing are conducted in landscapes of sometimes almost indescribable beauty and isolation. Little wonder then that Scotland exerts a irresistible magnetism which has aficionados returning year after year to enjoy some of the most spectacular sport in the world.

There is an enormous variety of feathered game to be found in Scotland, including pheasant, wild duck, partridge, woodcock and snipe. The red grouse, however, is the king of Scottish game birds and the Glorious Twelfth (of August) when the grouse season opens is a date treated with the reverence due the pinnacle of the shooting calendar. Notoriously fickle and vulnerable to a myriad of factors, grouse thrive on the young ling of open moorland on which guns can pay thousands of pounds for the privilege of taking part in a shoot.

The intensely romantic loneliness of the great Highland sporting estates is a perfect backdrop for stalking, a rugged and exhausting sport undertaken by those willing to spend hours and sometimes days on the hill, stalking their quarry and crawling when necessary through bog and heather to find the position for a perfect shot. It is predominantly red deer that are culled to improve herd quality and keep the population to numbers the estate deer forests can sustain. These "forests" appear to be a misnomer, being largely treeless, but derive their name from the great Caledonian pine forests which swathed the Highlands centuries ago. Stalking requires great patience and the not inconsiderable ability to keep up with the deceptively easy and unvarying pace of the stalker, whatever the terrain, without making sudden movements or more than the bare minimum of noise.

Salmon fishing in comparison is a sport of sublime contrasts. To stand in idyllic surroundings watching the fly fishing round is one of the most tranquil and soothing activities imaginable: then a great silver fish tears yards of line from the reel, the rod bows in resistance and the struggle begins. The best of Scotland's beautiful salmon rivers lie along the east coast, amongst them the Dee, Spey, Tay, Tweed, Conon and Helmsdale which remain legendary in the world of fly fishing despite the netting which has so badly damaged salmon stocks. During the season, the height of which is between July and September, salmon are fished on their return journey from the sea to the precise location at which they spawned, their unerring ability to find the spot dependant on infinitesimally minute concentrations of substances in the water which they can detect with their olfactory organs and follow. Supporting the somewhat unpopular and controversial theory that women are better salmon fishers than men, the largest salmon to have been caught on a rod and line was an enormous 64lb, hooked by a Miss Ballantine in October 1922. This magnificent fish came from the waters of the Tay, the middle beats of which are commanded by Kinnaird where the cast of one only slightly smaller at 50lb is displayed.

Aberdeenshire and Moray

Surrounded by the Grampians, the Cairngorms and the unforgiving North Sea, the landscapes of Aberdeenshire and Moray range from the uncompromising mountain scenery of the south and west to the plain but prosperous farmlands backing onto the forbidding north east littoral. Some of Scotland's finest salmon rivers, the Dee, Spey and Findhorn among them, run through the region, the peaty waters of which have made the "Golden Triangle" around Speyside the malt whisky capital of the world. Aberdeenshire and Moray are reputedly graced with more castles, standing and ruined, than any other county in Britain, while the legacy of the once powerful Picts is manifested in the many standing stones and hillforts throughout the area.

Aberdeen, built from locally hewn granite, is a prosperous if isolated metropolis lying on the east coast between the Dee and the Don. Love it or not, the grey and austere Granite City is transformed in sunshine by mica particles in the stone catching the light to merit the captivating description, "the great silver city by the golden sands."

In the sixth century St Machar was dispatched by St Columba to locate a "grassy platform near the sea, overlooking a river shaped like the crook on a bishop's crozier." Aberdeen fitted the not inconsiderable bill, a cathedral was built on the site and by the eleventh century the city had become one of the main royal residences of the Scottish kings. In the mid nineteenth century the speed of Aberdeen-built clippers gave Britain the leading edge in trade with China, tea being one of the less controversial cargos, and in 1882 the acquisition of steam tugboats propelled the fishing industry to countrywide prominence. Aberdeen is still an important fishing port, but its mainstay is without doubt the enormous and wealthy oil industry which has transformed the town since the first North Sea field opened in 1969.

South of Aberdeen is the town of Stonehaven, where on New Year's Day flaming balls are whirled overhead to ward off evil spirits in the ancient ceremony of

Fireballs. Celebrating Hogmanay, albeit on January 11th which is the end of the year according to the old calendar, Burghead on the north coast has another ancient fire ceremony in which a burning barrel of tar, the Clavie, is processed to the top of Dourie Hill and rolled down, broken fragments of the barrel being treasured as protection against the evil eye.

Just south of Stonehaven is the spectacular and almost surreal Dunnottar Castle. Besieged by Cromwell in the seventeenth century in search of, amongst other things, the Scottish Regalia, it was only the ingenuity of the local priest's wife, who smuggled it all to safety disguised as various household items, that prevented the unthinkable happening and the crown of Scotland physically falling into English hands.

Granite and roses
two emblems of Aberdeen

Running west from Aberdeen, Royal Deeside is scattered with a wonderful array of castles, many of them exquisite examples of Scottish baronial architecture. Balmoral, the Queen's summer residence, was originally bought by Queen Victoria in 1852 and completely remodelled in neo-baronial style according to plans drawn up by her beloved consort Albert. Set against an idyllic backdrop of forests and mountains and close to the beautiful River Dee, the attractions of Balmoral, whilst indisputable in the Queen's eyes, were at times somewhat lost on her guests. As one wrote, "It is very astonishing that the Royal power of England should reside amid this lonesome desolate cold mountain scenery."

Of the many castles in Deeside, Kildrummy, Drum and Craigievar illustrate fascinating early developments in Scottish castle architecture with great clarity. Kildrummy Castle, a romantic thirteenth century ruin where a Scottish blacksmith, bribed by the English to betray Robert the Bruce's family, was forced to drink his payment in the form of molten gold, is the most complete example of an early stone castle in Scotland. With an array of such newly devised features as an almost impregnable curtain wall, a gatehouse to protect the vulnerable entrance and an internal towerhouse for domestic quarters, Kildrummy was state of the art, an ultra modern fortress well equipped to cope with the increasingly sophisticated battle techniques of the thirteenth century.

Craigevar Castle
baronial architecture
at its finest

Drum Castle is entirely different structurally, built around one of the oldest tower houses in Scotland. Gifted by Robert the Bruce to his armour bearer after the Battle of Bannockburn in 1314, Drum was much expanded in the seventeenth century and remained in the same family for twenty four generations until the 1970's. In the turbulent years between the fourteenth and seventeenth centuries the vast majority of Scottish castles were built as tower houses, tall and thin, virtually windowless and thus easily defended.

Drum Castle

Typifying the next evolutionary stage from the basic tower house, Craigievar Castle is a wonderful confection of Scottish baronial architecture, a style which developed in the mid-sixteenth century. Although fortification remained a priority at ground level, extravagant embellishments and larger windows transformed the upper levels of the bleak and practical tower houses into fairytale palaces, of which Craigievar is an enchanting and almost unsurpassed example.

Just inland from the northern coast lies Elgin, a town of great loveliness and antiquity. The impressive remains of the episcopal Spynie Palace point to its mediaeval religious significance, from which time the street plan survives almost intact. Built in the thirteenth century, Elgin Cathedral was one of Scotland's most beautiful and important cathedrals and was described even then as "the glory of our Kingdom and the delight of foreigners." It was thus an appalling tragedy when the Wolf of Badenoch, illegitimate son of Robert II, and oblivious to the aesthetic value of the "Lantern of the North", all but destroyed the cathedral and town in 1390 in revenge for having been excommunicated by the Bishop for leaving his wife. Plundered during the Reformation by John Knox's similarly unappreciative Presbyterians and then a century later by Cromwell's men, the majestic cathedral was reduced to the magical ruins which still enhance Elgin today.

Whisky

Uisgebeatha, the Gaelic word for whisky, means water of life. The first records of whisky date from 1494 when James IV gave Friar John Cor some malted barley to make into aqua vitae. Whether the original know-how came from Irish monks or the Highlands is a moot point, but whatever its origin, whisky has graduated from its original medicinal purposes to become Scotland's most valuable export after oil.

The story of whisky is a fascinating reflection of social history. After Union with England in 1707, excessive duties imposed on whisky sparked such a lively trade in smuggling and illegal distillation that in 1777, of the four hundred and eight stills in Edinburgh, only eight were officially licensed. In 1780 a much vilified tax levied on claret boosted whisky consumption and, despite the arrest of a thousand "black" distillers in 1782, illegal trade flourished with the patriotic and vigorous support of all true Scots until in 1823 the Government bowed to the inevitable and relaxed the licensing laws. At the end of the nineteenth century phylloxera devastated the European vineyards and cognac with them, causing a whisky boom which lasted until American Prohibition in the 1920s. Since then, highly professional marketing and the fact that, despite attempts elsewhere, Scotland is the only country in the world that can make whisky have turned a romantic Scottish institution into a thriving £1 billion per year industry.

Single malt whisky is made from barley which is soaked in water and allowed to germinate, during which "malting" process starch in the grains becomes soluble and enzymes are produced to turn the starch into sugar. The barley is then dried over peat burners, mashed with hot water, at which stage the starch becomes sugar, and then subsequently fermented to convert the sugar to alcohol. After two distillations a colourless liquid is drawn off in a process requiring highly skilled judgement and matured for a minimum of three years in oak casks.

Good malts are matured for up to fourteen years and the distinctive flavour of a particular distillery's brand arises from an indefinable combination of the peat used for drying, the water for mashing, the oak in which it is matured and the magical "other" factor which endows Scottish whisky with its unique flavour and quality.

Single malts, the pure products of a specific distillery, are the ultimate in Scottish whiskies, inspiring an almost religious reverence in aficionados, whilst blends are made from single malts mixed with cheaper and easier to produce grain whiskies. Of the malt producing areas, Speyside and Islay are famed worldwide, the former for the unrivalled concentration of distilleries gathered in the "Golden Triangle", the latter for the peatiness and pungency of its malts.

The Highlands and Islands

For many, the wild and spectacular beauty of the Highlands and Islands embodies the very essence of Scotland. The majestic mountain scenery and abundance of vast empty spaces combine to create a spellbinding landscape, the loveliness of which almost defies belief. There are dazzling white sand beaches, glorious lochs and magnificent glens often bathed in a rain washed light of unparalleled brilliance and lucidity. Little wonder Robert Burns was inspired to write, "My heart's in the Highlands wherever I go."

The Highlands start in the Cairngorm mountains in the upper reaches of the Spey Valley. Separated from the Northern Highlands by the narrow lochs and fjords of the Great Glen, the inhospitable Cairngorms are clad in some of Britain's last native Caledonian pine forests. Towards the north, the gentle east coast gives way to a bleak terrain of lonely peat bogs, barren mountains and rugged seacliffs before turning south along what must be one of the most stunning coastlines in the world. The Islands lying to the west are similarly striking, and the entire breathtakingly beautiful region is home to some of the best fly fishing and stalking to be found anywhere in Britain or abroad.

The Highlands and Islands were frequently raided by the Vikings from the eighth century onwards, to the extent that much of the region was under Norse control until formally surrendered back to Scotland in 1266. The clan system became firmly established under the Vikings, and remained the basis of Highland life until the disaster of Culloden and the subsequent annihilation of the clan system due to English legislation and the cruel Highland Clearances. In these the clan chiefs, whose patriarchal obligations had been irrevocably eroded, ruthlessly evicted crofters from their land to make way for more lucrative sheep farming. Even now the central Highlands are virtually unpopulated, and scattered with forlorn ruins while the main centres of population lie around the coast.

Eilean Donnan Castle *guarding the road to the Isles in the Western Highlands*

Just east of Inverness is Drumossie Moor, scene of the Battle of Culloden in which Bonnie Prince Charlie's quest to restore the Stuart monarchy was finally and brutally ended by the "Butcher" Duke of Cumberland in 1746. The massacre lasted for just over an hour, after which Bonnie Prince Charlie fled through the Highlands to Skye, whence he sailed to permanent exile. His escape was a magnificent tribute to the loyalty of the desperately poor Highlanders, given the English booty of £30,000 on his head.

Half a century later, the Sutherland estate in the far north of the Highlands was the scene of some of the most savage Clearances of the nineteenth century. The Dukes of Sutherland were among the greatest landowners in Europe and their lack of compassion for the crofters generated a bitterness that still exists. The Castle of Dunrobin, seat of the Sutherlands, is one of Scotland's largest ancestral homes, a magical flight of fantasy designed by the architect of the Houses of Parliament and loosely based on the Châteaux of the Loire. Queen Victoria described

Ben Loyal
across the waters of Loch Loyal

Balmoral as simple in comparison, such was its grandeur and magnificence. It was, no doubt, a far cry from the bleak living conditions of the dispossessed, some of whom were relocated to Bettyhill, a village created on the exposed north coast and modestly named after Elizabeth, Countess of Sutherland.

At the Fort William end of the Great Glen, below the unforgettable white beaches and exquisite scenery of the western shoreline, lies the eerily beautiful Glen Coe where one of the vilest episodes in Scottish history took place. William of Orange, under whose auspices Fort William was built, ordered that the Campbells lodge with Clan MacDonald and in the dead of night murder all those younger than 70 for the crime of being a few days late signing an obligatory, if meaningless, oath of allegiance to him. For the honourable Highlanders the real shame of the Massacre of Glen Coe lay not so much in the crime itself, bloodshed being more or less part of everyday life in those troubled times, but in the unforgiveable abuse of clan hospitality.

The clans, if unruly on the mainland, operated as virtually autonomous monarchs in the Islands off the west coast of Scotland. Once dominated by the Lords of the Isles, Skye and the archipelago of the Western Isles (Outer Hebrides) still fiercely maintain their Celtic roots to the extent that Gaelic is the first language for many islanders. The island lifestyle is inextricably bound up with a distinctive form of Hebridean Presbyterianism, strictly Calvinistic and rigid in its observation of the Sabbath. This is particularly so in the Western Isles of Lewis, Harris and North Uist, where in some areas even the children's swings are padlocked on Sundays. Only the southernmost Western Isles of Barra and South Uist were unaffected by the Reformation and remain somewhat more relaxed in their Catholicism.

The islands are, without exception, compelling in their isolated and windswept beauty. Skye is dominated by the Cuillins, a range of jagged snow clad peaks which rise dramatically from sea level, the sight of which from Elgol is reputedly one of the most spectacular views in Britain. In the north of the island are the ruins of Dunvegan Castle, seat of the MacLeods for seven hundred years, whose discourtesy to St Columba led the mountains of the neighbouring Duinnish Peninsula to shed their peaks in shame, so legend has it, and be known henceforth as the MacLeod Tables. Bonnie Prince Charlie's last moments on Scottish soil were spent on Skye, due to the courage of Flora MacDonald, who smuggled him there "over the sea" from Benbecula disguised as her maid.

Relentlessly buffeted by the Atlantic waves and winds, the myriad Western Isles have a lonely romanticism borne of their isolation and wondrous landscapes of perfect golden sands, brooding heather clad mountains and steaming peat bogs. Lewis, the largest of the islands, has been inhabited since 4000 BC and the Standing Stones of Callanish, one of Scotland's most atmospheric and intriguing prehistoric ruins, date from the Bronze Age Beaker People of 3000 to 1500 BC. The round coastal fortification of Carloway Broch was built by the Celts, probably around 400 BC, whilst the Viking legacy is manifested in the fact that four out of five place names in Lewis are still of Nordic origin.

Geographically connected to Lewis but distinct from it after a rift in the MacLeod
clan, Harris was the birthplace of the Harris Tweed industry, set up during the
famine of the nineteenth century when the Countess of Dunmore sold surplus
cloth to her sporting aristocratic friends. The incomparable scenery of Harris,
with its pristine silver beaches and turquoise waters dominated by a mountain
backdrop, is perhaps the ultimate in Scotland's uplifting Highland landscapes.

Sunset on Harris

Orkney and The Shetlands

Lying off northern Scotland and bearing the full brunt of the fearsome winter storms are the remote archipelagos of Orkney and the Shetlands. Although very different from each other and determinedly separate from mainland Scotland, both owe much of their character and culture to six centuries of Nordic domination.

The islands of Orkney are only six miles from north east Scotland. Mostly fertile and low lying, with the exception of Hoy in which mountainous moorland plunges abruptly a thousand feet to the sea, the warming influence of the Gulf Stream endows both Orkney and Shetland with a mild, if hectic, climate which belies their northerly latitude.

This hospitable environment proved a magnet for settlers from Neolithic times and Orkney's ancient history is vividly related through a plethora of prehistoric sites and ancient stones, all of which exude a compelling and powerful aura of antiquity. On Mainland, Orkney's largest island, the atmospheric and architecturally awe-inspiring burial chamber of Maes Howe dates from 3500 BC, whilst the oldest stone houses in Europe lie on Papa Westray. Skara Brae is a Stone Age settlement, swamped by sand 4,500 years ago and thus wonderfully preserved until a violent storm exposed a tantalising glimpse of what lay below in 1850. Orkney then, as now, was virtually treeless and the enduring if excruciatingly uncomfortable qualities of the stone furniture found at the site quite defy contemplation.

A hundred miles north of Scotland and subject to more violent weather than anywhere else in the British Isles, The Shetlands are bleaker than Orkney and surrounded by a dramatic coastline which bears testament to the battle of the elements continually waged about its shores.

Most of the Shetlands' population regards itself as more Nordic than Scottish and the influence of the islands' Norse heritage is flamboyantly illustrated in "Up-Helly-Aa" a theatrical fire festival heralding the return of the sun at the end

Orkney *basalt cliffs confront the might of the North Atlantic*

of January. Clad in winged helmet and shining armour, flame bearers process behind a Viking longship, which is eventually torched signalling the start of a night of riotous carnival.

Shetland's long maritime history was never more clandestine than during World War II when the Shetland "Bus" ferried arms and resistance workers between Shetland and Norway in conditions of appalling danger. Their position at the gale-ridden gateway between the North Sea and North Atlantic has made the islands a

welcome refuge for shipping over the years and the baronial style Town Hall of Lerwick was donated to the islanders by Norway, Holland and Germany in gratitude for kindnesses shown to seamen over the years.

Like Orkney, the Shetlands are an anthropological treasure trove, and the extraordinary Jarlshof, in which settlement after settlement was built on the same site, constitutes one of the most condensed synopses of history to be found anywhere in the world.

Ring of Brodgar
prehistoric remains on Orkney

Picture credits

Photographs

p1 Doug Corrance p4 Glyn Satterley p5 Bill Roberton p7 David Robertson
p8 David Robertson p17 Ken Paterson p20 STB p22 David Robertson p25 Angus Johnston
p29 S J Taylor p33 Paul Tomkins/STB p34 Doug Corrance p35 Derek Laird p36 STB
p39 Paul Tomkins/STB p41 Doug Corrance p42 STB p45 STB p47 Glyn Satterley
p48 Paul Tomkins/STB p53 Stephen Kearney p54 C Paterson p57 STB p58 Peter Davenport
p61 David Robertson p62 Doug Corrance p63 G Summers p64 Harvey Wood
p67 Robert Lees p68 Doug Corrance p71 Robert Lees p73 Robert Lees p74 Pinhole
Productions p76 STB p77 Robert E Walker p78 Peter Davenport p81 Paul Tomkins/STB
p82 Doug Corrance p83 Harvey Wood p84 Harvey Wood p87 David Robertson
pp88/89 David Robertson p91 Stephen Kearney p93 David Robertson pp94/95 Glyn Satterley

Source: The Still Moving Picture Company, Edinburgh

Reproductions

p12 The Royal Collection © Her Majesty The Queen
pp14, 15, 19, 27, 50 National Galleries of Scotland

Declaration of Arbroath

Courtesy of the Scottish Record Office SP13/7 ©HMSO

Ptarmigan Publishing Ltd
Ptarmigan House
No 9 The Coda Centre
189 Munster Road
London SW6 6AW
Telephone: 0171-381 5600
Facsimile: 0171-381 4012

Printed by Sceptre Litho, Leicester

HOTELS
of
DISTINCTION

London ❖ Scotland ❖ Ireland

Hotels of Distinction 1998

Published by
Ptarmigan Publishing Ltd
Growers Court, New Road, Bromham,
Chippenham, Wiltshire, SN15 2JA

For sales and branding opportunities
call Frangelica O'Shea or Hugh Roche

Telephone   01380 - 859983
Facsimile   01380 - 859682

© 1998 Ptarmigan Publishing Ltd

Managing Director   Mark Hodson
Production Director   Mark Dawson
Marketing Director   Frangelica O'Shea
Sales Manager   Hugh Roche

Printed in England by Sceptre Litho, Leicester
Colour origination by Sceptre Litho, Leicester

Distributed in the UK by
Macmillan Distribution Ltd
Houndsmills, Basingstoke, Hampshire, RG21 6XS

Welcome to Hotels of Distinction 1998. As our title promises, each of the hotels featured in these pages was approached by us because it possesses some distinctive quality. Excellence of service certainly, but not exclusively - it might also be a spectacular Highland view from your bedroom, fascinating historic associations, wonderful cuisine, or unique leisure facilities. We are extremely grateful to all the hotels who have supported us and made such a resounding success of our first issue.

This 1998 launch issue of Hotels of Distinction is distributed free with every copy of Past & Present London, Scotland, and Ireland. In 1999, Hotels of Distinction will feature hotels throughout the entire UK, and will also provide a comprehensive overview of attractions and leisure opportunities in the region. We aim to become the essential reference for the discerning visitor to these islands.

We hope the following pages and the accompanying Past & Present titles help to bring out the best of London, Scotland, and Ireland.

Mark Hodson

London

Scotland

Ireland

 135 rooms — Total number of rooms

 Tennis court

 Tranquil location

 Golf courses on site or nearby

 Chef/Patron

 At least one no-smoking bedroom

 Children welcome (minimum age where applicable)

 Pets accommodated in rooms or kennels (GDO: guide dogs only)

 Lift available for guests' use

 Riding can be arranged

 Excellent and comprehensive wine list

 Fishing can be arranged

 Four poster bed available

 Shooting can be arranged

 Cable/satellite TV in all bedrooms

 Hotel has a helicopter landing pad

 Direct-dial telephone in all bedrooms

 Licensed for wedding ceremonies

 Meeting/conference facilities (max. no. delegates)

 Wheelchair access to at least one bedroom and public rooms

(The 'access for wheelchairs' symbol does not necessarily indicate that the property fulfils National Accessible Scheme grading)

 Swimming pool

London

Through the millennia London has seen many changes. From Celtic settlement to outpost of imperial Rome; from mediaeval seaport to hub of an empire that spanned the globe. And throughout the ages it has been a magnet for the enterprising and ambitious, both from within the UK and from overseas, who have helped maintain its place among the great cities of the world.

London may no longer be the first capital among nations - others have earned the right to claim that crown - but it has lost little of its former glory, and in recent years has added new lustre to its reputation. For those who love to shop it is one of the world's great bazaars, affording everything from the prestigious premises of the West End through a cornucopia of specialist outlets to its many colourful and fascinating street markets. Eating out offers a similarly bewildering choice: London offers probably the widest variety of authentic ethnic cuisines afforded by any city, ample and welcome evidence of the many populations from around the world who have made London their home. Always a centre for music, whether contemporary or classical, it is now also taking the lead where others once ruled the field; Paris now imports London's fashion ideas, its architects and designers lead the field in the hunt for international commissions, and the city is now acknowledged as among the leading locations in the world for innovative haute cuisine.

A city of many faces and historic traditions, where panoply and pageant play a daily part, London today is looking boldly towards the future.

Month	Event	Venue
January		
January 1	London Parade	Parliament Square SW1 to Berkeley Square W1
January 9-18	London International Boat Show	Earl's Court, SW5
January 21-25	Art '98, The London Contemporary Art Fair	Business Design Centre, N1
January 22- April 13	Art Treasures of England Exhibition	Royal Academy of Arts, W1
February		
February 1	Chinese New Year Celebrations	Soho W1
February 1-8	Benson and Hedges Masters Snooker Tournament	Wembley Conference Centre
February 24 - March 1	Fine Arts & Antiques Fair	Olympia, W14
March		
March 19-29	Chelsea Antiques Fair	Chelsea Old Town Hall, SW3
March 19 - June 14	Icons from Russia Exhibition	Royal Academy of Arts, Piccadilly W1
March 28	Beefeater Gin Oxford & Cambridge Boat Race	Putney to Mortlake, River Thames
April		
April 26	Flora International Marathon 1998	Greenwich to The Mall
May		
May 2	Rugby League Challenge Cup Final	Wembley Stadium
May 9	Rugby, Pilkington Cup Final	Twickenham, Middlesex
May 13-17	Royal Windsor Horse Show	Home Park, Windsor
May 16	FA Challenge Cup Final	Wembley Stadium
May 19-22	Chelsea Flower Show	Royal Hospital, Chelsea
June		
June 3-4	Beating Retreat - Massed Bands of the Household Division	Horse Guards Parade
June 6	Derby Day	Epsom Race Course, Surrey
June 7 - August 16	Royal Academy Summer Exhibition	Royal Academy of Arts, Piccadilly
June 8-14	Stella Artois Tennis Championships	Queen's Club, W14
June 9-11	Beating Retreat - Massed Bands of the Royal Artillery	Horse Guards Parade
June 13	The Queen's Birthday Parade - Trooping of the Colour	Horse Guards Parade
June 16-19	Ascot Race Meeting	Ascot, Berkshire
June 22 - July 5	Wimbledon Lawn Tennis Championships	All England Club, SW9
July		
July 1-5	International Henley Royal Regatta	Henley-on-Thames, Oxfordshire
July 21 - August 21	Royal Tournament	Earls Court, SW5
August		
August 30-31	Notting Hill Carnival	Ladbroke Grove, W10
September		
September 7-13	Farnborough International Air Show	Farnborough Airfield, Hampshire
September 23-27	Horse of the Year Show	Wembley Arena, Wembley
October		
October 29 - November 1	Kensington Fine Art & Antiques Fair	Kensington Town Hall, W8
November		
November 1	RAC London to Brighton Veteran Car Run	Hyde Park, W2
November 5	Guy Fawkes Night	
November 8	Remembrance Day Wreath Laying Ceremony	Cenotaph, Whitehall SW1
November 14	Lord Mayor's Show	City of London
December		
December 17-21	International Showjumping Championships	Olympia, W14
December 24	Christmas Eve Service	Westminster Abbey
December 31	New Years Eve Celebrations	Trafalgar Square

The most *elegant beds*

IN THE WORLD

BY THE LATER PART OF THIS CENTURY Classical French beds, widely admired for two hundred years, had become virtually unobtainable. Simon Horn created his company in 1982 to redress this situation, thereby both inspiring and guiding a resurgence of interest in these masterpieces of design and craftsmanship. Today, as designers, manufacturers, and retailers, Simon Horn are the acknowledged leaders in the field providing a unique collection of some seventy different designs ranging from austere simplicity to ornate splendour.

Bespoke...

Each pattern has its own carefully-researched and validated provenance, drawing on many years' accumulated expertise and knowledge of an eclectic variety of sources. Although strictly faithful to the spirit of the original, the service is truly bespoke. Dimensions can be altered, headboards and footboards can be raised, lowered or removed, frames can be carved, caned, upholstered, panelled, veneered or painted, with a selection of fine woods and finishes to suit different tastes and budgets, and high quality mattresses specially made to fit all sizes.

Much of the work is undertaken in the company's workshop in Devon, with other facilities sourced from craftsmen overseas, taking advantage of local skills and techniques from a range of resources from rural France to Kashmir. The result is a piece of furniture built to the same exacting standards as its antique forebear, and with the same qualities of beauty, craftsmanship and durability: an antique in all but age.

Those requiring a bed in a hurry, or for whom an example exactly fits the bill, can simply purchase one of the many beds held in stock at the showrooms. Visitors are invited to examine for themselves the qualities which distinguish a truly great bed, and see these same standards applied to other items of traditional English and Provincial French furniture, from small occasional tables to chairs, desks, armoires and dining tables.

Built by craftsmen using the world's finest natural materials, made to last for centuries

...and designed for life

A cot for a baby ...

... a bed for a child ...

... a sofa for life.

The unique Simon Horn Cot draws its inspiration from the 18th Century concept of 'metamorphic' furniture. From birth to adulthood, the same piece evolves and finds new purpose: first a cot, then a bed, finally a sofa, exhibiting grace and beauty in all its incarnations. Crafted to the same exacting standards as all Simon Horn furniture and available in a variety of styles, the Simon Horn Cot has been awarded a British Standards Institute Certificate for the ingenuity of its patented design.

**Simon Horn
Furniture Limited**
117-121 Wandsworth
Bridge Road
London SW6 2TP

Tel: 0171-731 1279
Fax: 0171-736 3522

HOME *thoughts*

LADY DAPHNE IS MORE THAN JUST a shop - it stimulates new ways of looking at homes and living.

In beautiful and historic premises where Sloane Street meets Sloane Square, Lady Daphne will inspire exciting new ideas about home furnishing, decoration and interior design and gifts that will be remembered. From leather goods to china, fashion accessories to children's items, silver to furniture: all bear its distinctive mark of quality of production and clarity of design. Most of the items to be found are available nowhere else; many are designed and created exclusively for Lady Daphne by its own craftsmen, and can be produced to your specification to suit your environment.

Destined to become the antiques of the future, Lady Daphne's merchandise and ideas regularly attract leading interior designers and interior shops. A growing list of international clients make a visit to Lady Daphne an essential part of their London stopover, and friendly, helpful, and knowledgeable staff are there to help you make the hardest decision of all: what to leave behind until next time.

Lady Daphne is England's leading manufacturer of Toleware

Lady Daphne

145 Sloane Street
Sloane Square
London SW1X 9AY
Tel: 0171 - 730 1131
Fax: 0171 - 730 1141

Pantalon Chameleon

Pantalon Chameleon's distinctive own label for highest quality leather and suede trousers, skirts and jackets.

ARCADIAN *splendour*

Discreetly hidden in the heart of London's most exclusive shopping district, the elegant Georgian passage of glass and wood that is *Burlington Arcade* links Bond Street to St James' in one of the world's most prestigious retail addresses.

Ever since the early nineteenth century its magnificent architectural setting and prime location have attracted some of London's most exclusive shops. Today, *Burlington Arcade* is famous throughout the world for the range and quality of leather goods, benchmade shoes, jewellery, cashmere, perfume and gifts available in the 40 shops found beneath its vaulted roof.

For London's finest range of presents, try shopping from the past. It's an experience to treasure.

Perfume
toiletries
by The Crown Perfumery

Benchmade shoes
classic brogue
by Church's

Jewellery
from Tim Watkins

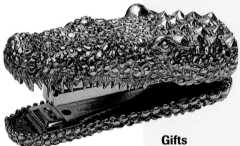

Gifts
pewter crocodile stapler
from Royal Selangor

Cashmere
lacy look knitted vest top
with matching cardigan
by N Peal

Leather goods
overnight bags in
soft dressed bridle
by Pickett

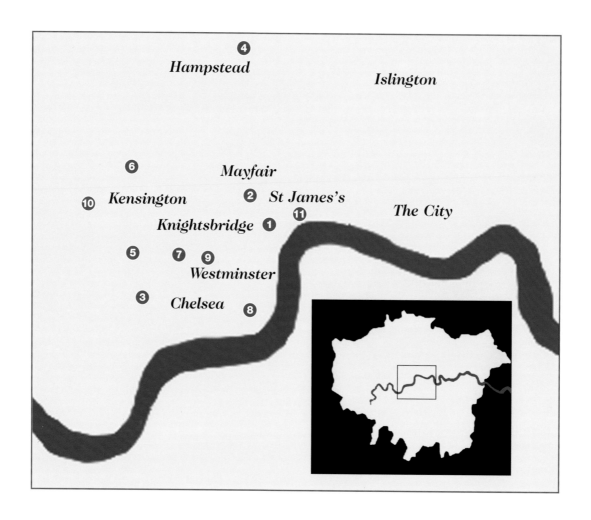

The Stafford

Executive Director: **Terry Holmes**

Situated alongside Green Park in St James's, The Stafford is a consummate expression of the understated elegance, quality, and impeccable service for which this area of central London has long been a byword. Guest rooms and suites are individually furnished in the style of a traditional London townhouse but with all the modern amenities expected of a top class hotel. The Carriage House, built in the eighteenth century as stables and now converted into spacious guest rooms and suites, retains many of the stable's original features while enjoying the same high standard of service and amenities.

Fine food and wine will figure largely in any stay at The Stafford, where an award-winning team of chefs create a range of modern, British, and classical dishes to satisfy all palates, complemented by a vast selection of rare and fine vintages. In the world-famous American Bar the drinks are long, the conversation lively, and the light fare always delicious.

The Stafford, St James's Place, London SW1A 1NJ
Tel: 0171 - 493 0111   Fax: 0171 - 493 7121
E-mail: info@thestaffordhotel.co.uk

80 rooms

S: £199
D: £220 - £310   **Suites:**   from £330

Ascott Mayfair

General Manager: Christine Malcolm

Situated between Park Lane and Berkeley Square in the fashionable heart of London, a short walk from Bond Street, Piccadilly, and St James', the Ascott Mayfair provides a luxurious alternative to the traditional hotel. Guests are invited to select from a choice of apartments accommodating up to six people and decorated in an elegant and refined art deco style which reflects the period of the property's original development. Each of the Ascott Mayfair's 56 suites affords an entirely private environment with a fully equipped kitchen and state of the art amenities, including music systems, fax, modem points, VCR and satellite TV, and direct dial telephones with voice mail.

Rates include a daily maid service and breakfast in The Terrace overlooking the private landscaped garden. Throughout the Ascott Mayfair, a meticulous and highly personalised attention to detail ensures that guests enjoy the relaxed atmosphere, comfort, and intimacy of a private home. Concierge, private boardroom and executive support services are all to a standard expected of the very highest class of hotel. The Club, a lounge and bar exclusively for

residents and their guests, and the Hothouse health club add to the Ascott Mayfair's attractions as an independent base in one of London's most prestigious locations.

Ascott Mayfair, 49 Hill Street, Mayfair, London W1X 7FQ
Tel: 0171 - 499 6868   Fax: 0171 - 499 0705
E-mail: ascottmf@scotts.com.sg

56 suites

Studio: £164 - £180   **2 bed:** £375 - £395
1 bed: £247 - £265   **3 bed:** £485 - £510

Blakes

Group General Manager: Jonathan Critchard

Each of the 52 bedrooms was individually designed by Anouska Hempel to her own uncompromising standards. Interiors blend Russian, Eastern European, Colonial, and Turkish influences to stunning effect, creating a caravanserai in which the resting traveller of the global trade routes can enjoy the convenience and high-tech efficiency of modern living amid princely splendour. On the ground floor the courtyard garden, lush with greenery throughout the year, provides a similarly secluded refuge.

Blakes restaurant, presenting a skilful blend of western and oriental traditions complemented by a magnificent wine list, has become one of the most sought-after tables in London, with diners regularly including many of those leading lights of the creative world who select Blakes hotel for its privacy and discretion. Above all, the ever critical and creative eye of its owner ensures that Blakes continues to provide a unique sense of excitement and adventure.

Blakes was created just over ten years ago, and at the time the style and ambience conceived by its owner Anouska Hempel, the internationally renowned British designer, was considered breathtakingly daring as a concept for a world-class hotel. Today Blakes continues in a class of its own, but has established a benchmark which the "fashionable small hotel" around the world strives to match.

Blakes Hotel, 33 Roland Gardens, London SW7 3PF
Tel: 0171 - 370 6701   Fax: 0171 - 373 0442
E-mail: blakes@easynet.co.uk

52 rooms

S: £130
D: £155 - £300   **Suites:**   £475 - £695

The Sandringham

General Manager: Diana Sparks

The Sandringham Hotel, located in the sought-after residential area of Hampstead Village, is a private country house hotel occupying an elegant Victorian mansion. The drawing and dining rooms are classically furnished, while the beautiful walled garden provides an additional and tranquil setting for afternoon tea or an evening drink. Each of the seventeen bedrooms has been individually designed, with fine fabrics and furnishings combining to create a welcoming atmosphere of home comfort which extends throughout the hotel.

The day starts with a magnificent breakfast, featuring freshly squeezed juices, home-baked breads and, for heartier appetites, sizzling hot dishes. An extensive range of catering facilities and services can be provided, with receptions, seminars, dinner parties or afternoon teas all organised with the same creativity and attention to detail. For those attending meetings or planning a day's sightseeing, Hampstead's underground station is a mere five minutes' walk, giving quick and easy access to all parts of central London. For guests interested in a morning jog or afternoon walk, entry to Hampstead Heath (a famous 950 acre area of gently contoured woodland) is ten minutes' walk from the Sandringham's front door.

Sandringham Hotel, 3 Holford Road, Hampstead Village, London NW3 1AD
Tel: 0171 - 435 1569   Fax: 0171 - 431 5932

S:	£70 - £85		
D:	£115 - £130	**Suites:**	£145 - £155

Millennium Bailey's Hotel

General Manager: Olivia Hetherington

The Millennium Bailey's Hotel, originally opened in 1876, has recently been renovated and carefully restored to its original glory. Complemented by its elegant facade, Bailey's now offers the comforts of a luxurious home with the convenience of modern hotel facilities and traditional service. All 212 bedrooms and suites are individual and include en suite bathrooms, air conditioning, fax/modem points, 240/110 voltage, and 24 hour in room dining.

Olives restaurant and bar offers an unusual menu combining traditional English and modern contemporary dishes. The surroundings are informal minimalist which sit comfortably with the 19th century architecture of Bailey's. The Conservatory, London's only all glass venue, offers a variety of light meals and drinks throughout the day and provides entertainment each evening.

Bailey's is located in the most favoured residential area of the Royal Borough of Kensington and Chelsea and, unusually for London, has its own car park. Bailey's is opposite Gloucester Road tube station which is served by the Circle, District, and Piccadilly lines giving direct links with the City, theatreland, and London's finest museums.

Bailey's Hotel, 140 Gloucester Road, London SW7 4QH
Tel: 0171 - 373 6000   Fax: 0171 - 370 3760
E-mail: baileys@mill-cop.com

212 rooms

S: £135
D: £195

Suites: £250

The Hempel

General Manager: **Barry Polson**

In creating The Hempel, Anouska Hempel's latest hotel after the ground-breaking Blakes, a row of white Georgian houses has been transformed into a haven of contemplative calm. Elegant spaces are washed by ever-changing light and shade, elements combine in restful harmony; once inside, the visitor participates in a new and inspirational definition of luxury. Each of the rooms and public areas has been designed in sympathy with The Hempel's guiding principle of creating an environment that reflects and sustains inner tranquillity, which finds its perfect expression in the hotel's Zen garden: yet each room sustains the needs of the modern traveller with three telephones, fax and modem facilities, CD and video player, air conditioning, even oxygen in the mini-bar. Four function rooms, private dining rooms, video conferencing facilities, libraries, fitness rooms and private apartments all subscribe to the same ethos.

The I-Thai restaurant exemplifies The Hempel's synthesis of classical Eastern and Western traditions with a menu that blends the finest of Italian, Thai, and Japanese influences. The Shadow Bar delights even the visual appetite by casting shadows over diners, creating illusions redolent of Oriental philosophy. With the personal service and

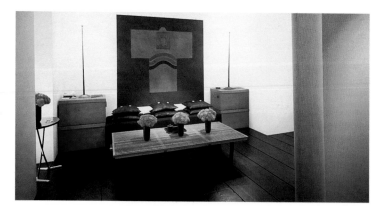

attention to the highest standards that have become Anouska Hempel's hallmark, The Hempel more than any other hotel lies beyond description, and can only be appreciated by experience.

The Hempel, Hempel Garden Square, 31-35 Craven Hill Gardens, London W2 3EA
Tel: 0171 - 298 9000   Fax: 0171 - 402 4666
E-mail: the-hempel@easynet.co.uk

41
rooms

D: from £220
Suites: from £370

Number Sixteen

General Manager: **Jean Branham**

Virtually unaltered from the days of its early Victorian origins, the immaculate pillared façade of Number Sixteen is the gateway to a haven of calm and seclusion in South Kensington. In winter an open fire in the comfortably informal drawing room entices with its warmth; in summer the conservatory opens into the enclosed garden, a regular award-winner for the beauty of its floral displays. In the library, a perfect setting for greeting friends or for an informal business meeting, visitors are invited to pour themselves a drink from the honour bar.

The bedrooms have been tastefully and individually decorated with a discreet combination of antiques and traditional furnishings: all have a private bathroom, colour television, hair dryer, personal bar, clock radio, and direct-dial telephone. Breakfast is served in the comfort and privacy of your room.

Throughout the hotel, the friendly and attentive service of Number Sixteen's staff ensures that visitors are looked after as if guests in a private home. The hotel is a short walk away from some of the best restaurants, pubs, and shops in London, with the nearby South Kensington underground station providing easy access to the West End and City, and a direct link to Heathrow airport.

Number Sixteen, 16 Sumner Place, London SW7 3EG
Tel: 0171- 589 5232   Fax: 0171 - 584 8615
US Toll-free Tel: 1800 592 5387
E-mail: Reservations@NumberSixteenHotel.co.uk

 36 rooms

S: £85 - £120
D: £155 - £185   **Suites:** £195

Dolphin Square Hotel

Hotel Operations Manager: **Clare Stewart**

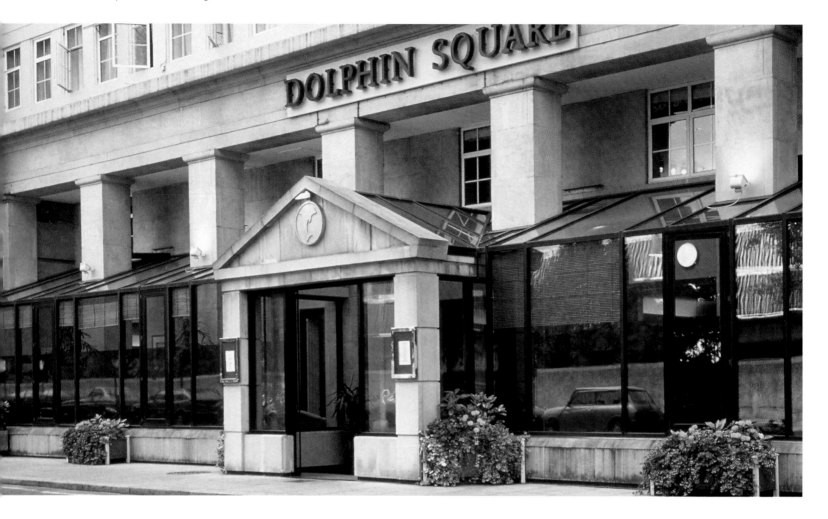

One of London's few all suite establishments, Dolphin Square sets out to provide its guests with all the benefits of a high quality central London hotel, but with value for money equally in mind. Set within 3.5 acres of gardens in Pimlico a few minutes walk from Westminster Abbey and the Houses of Parliament, a suite in Dolphin Square represents an oasis of space and comfort in the heart of London.

Each of the attractive and spacious suites comprises a comfortable sitting room with cable TV and direct dial telephones, a fully fitted kitchen, and up to three bedrooms. Each benefits from the full range of facilities available at Dolphin Square, including the Health Club with its famous 60ft indoor pool, gym, brasserie, bar, shops, travel agency and theatre booking service, on-site parking, dry cleaning and laundry service. Room service provides a range of food and drink from breakfast to late at night.

The Dolphin Square business centre offers a full range of secretarial and communications services complementing conference and event facilities capable of serving from 6 to 80 delegates. With excellent access to the West End and City, and also with Heathrow and

Gatwick airports, Dolphin Square represents the ideal location for the corporate traveller.

Dolphin Square, Chichester Street, London SW1V 3LX

Tel: 0171 - 798 8890   Fax: 0171 - 798 8896

E-mail: dolphinsq@btinternet.com

S: £100
D: £135   **Suites:**   £180

Cliveden Town House

General Manager: Stephen Colley

As its name suggests, The Cliveden Town House is the metropolitan cousin of Cliveden, formerly one of Britain's most celebrated country residences and now perhaps the finest hotel in the country. Overlooking a leafy square between Chelsea and Knightsbridge, enjoying peaceful seclusion yet within easy reach of the West End and City, The Town House matches the assured charm and elegant proportions of its Edwardian setting with the most demanding of contemporary standards of service and efficiency.

Air conditioning, private facsimile, voice mail, satellite TV, and a complete audio and video system in each of the bedrooms answer modern needs; open fires, twenty four hour room service, the relaxing drawing room and library, and the luxury of The Town House's specially-specified bedlinen and oversized beds reflect an equally exacting standard of domestic service and attentiveness to the needs and comfort of guests.

Designed and managed by the same team which established Cliveden as one of the world's top hotels, The Cliveden Town House above all else sets out to provide its guests with a haven of comfort and luxury in the heart of the city, applying the same attentiveness to detail and consideration to its guests' every possible need as at its rural counterpart.

The Cliveden Town House, 26 Cadogan Gardens, London SW3 2RP
Tel: 0171 - 730 6466   Fax: 0171 - 730 0236

rooms **35**

S:	£120 - £180
D:	£210 - £250

Suites: £310 - £620

Royal Garden Hotel

General Manager: **Graham Bamford**

After its £30 million refurbishment the Royal Garden Hotel in Kensington is one of Britain's most prestigious five star hotels - the perfect venue for a luxurious stay in fashionable Kensington.

As its name suggests the Royal Garden is a close neighbour of Kensington Palace, its situation alongside Kensington Gardens affording sweeping views of London across the park. With the best of London's museums, fashion boutiques, antique markets and the Royal Albert Hall only a short walk away, access by public transport or taxi to the West End or City is equally advantageous. Amongst the hotel's facilities are the informal Park Terrace Restaurant, offering an extensive menu in a relaxing environment, and the stylish The Tenth bar and restaurant which commands stunning panoramic views of the London skyline across Hyde Park.

The hotel boasts 400 rooms including 30 suites, with a wide range of facilities and amenities including satellite TV with in-house movies, mini bar, and direct-dial telephones with voice mail. Boardroom and function facilities are among the largest and most flexible in London: the Palace Suite accommodates 400 guests for a dinner dance, while the more intimate atmosphere of the Kensington Suite is perfect for smaller meetings or events.

Royal Garden Hotel, 2-24 Kensington High Street, London W8 4PT
Tel: 0171 - 937 8000   Fax: 0171 - 361 1991
E-mail: sales@royalgdn.co.uk

400

S: £195

D: £235   **Suites:** from £335

The Howard

General Manager: Nicolino Martini

On the Embankment overlooking the Thames where the City meets the West End, The Howard commands a magnificent view of the river from St Paul's Cathedral to the Houses of Parliament with many of London's prime attractions within short walking distance. At The Howard, location, decor, facilities, service, and cuisine marry together to the advantage of leisure and business traveller alike.

Ornate eighteenth century ceilings and decorative Adam style friezes combine with marble pillars and glittering chandeliers to create an atmosphere of imperial splendour, while bedrooms feature French marquetry furniture and marble bathrooms.

Modern needs are equally well provided in all bedrooms, and include a valet service, air conditioning, 24 hour room service, satellite and CNN channels and direct-dial telephones, while the Business Centre provides a comprehensive rage of services for the executive guest including boardroom facilities. The Temple Bar creates a relaxing and stylish rendezvous in which to enjoy a cocktail prior to lunch or dinner in the celebrated Quai d'Or restaurant, both of which overlook a garden terrace. Four conference rooms are available, the smallest being the Surrey and Westminster suites, which overlook the River Thames and are ideal for luncheon or dinner parties, while the Fitzalan and Arundel cater for up to 200 persons.

The Howard, Temple Place, The Strand, London WC2R 2PR
Tel: 0171 - 836 3555   Fax: 0171 - 379 4547
E-mail: reservations@thehowardhotel.co.uk

135 rooms

S: £255
D: £285   **Suites:**   £305 - £565

Out of Town

When a man is tired of London, he is tired of life;
for there is in London all that life can afford.

Samuel Johnson's words are as true today as they have ever been, yet even the most ardent lover of city life will agree that a short break can add new spice to any relationship.

One of the great charms of the UK for many of its foreign visitors is its economy of scale: for those accustomed to lands built on more generous lines, the UK seems to present an immense amount of history crammed into a very small space. A short trip by car or train from London brings the whole of Southern England within your grasp. Ancient cities - Bath, Salisbury, Winchester, Oxford - unspoilt countryside, historic castles and great houses, world-renowned sites of prehistory such as Stonehenge and Avebury, all are within easy reach.

Yet even better is the opportunity to spend a few nights in peaceful seclusion, recharging the batteries before the next foray into the great wen. The opportunity also to enjoy a base from which to explore the South, for twenty centuries the economic and political heart of England.

The Queensberry

Proprietors: **Stephen and Penny Ross**

Built by John Wood to the Marquis of Queensberry's commission, this elegant property located in a quiet residential street in central Bath now houses an intimate town house hotel. The Regency stucco ceilings, ornate cornices and panelling of its interior enchantingly complement the harmonious strength of the facade of this classic example from the golden age of Georgian architecture. The private rooms and suites, each individually decorated under the direction of Penny Ross, enjoy en suite bathrooms, room service, and state of the art office support for executives. The hotel's informal Olive Tree Restaurant, in which proprietor Stephen Ross enthusiastically exercises his distinctive culinary arts in the preparation of the best of contemporary cooking, is deservedly one of the most sought-after tables in an area blessed with a very high standard of cuisine. A quiet walled garden provides an additional restful oasis for the visitor to the Queensberry.

Situated at the heart of Bath, The Queensberry provides a haven of tranquillity close to the Circus and Assembly Rooms and a short walk from the many fascinating and historic splendours of the only city to be listed by UNESCO as a World Heritage Site.

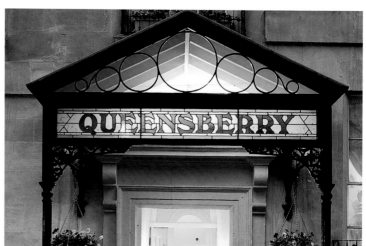

Location: Russel Street is opposite the Assembly Rooms off Bennett St

The Queensberry, Russel Street, Bath, Bath & NE Somerset BA1 2QF
Tel: 01225 447928   Fax: 01225 446065
E-mail: queensberry@dial.pipex.com

27 rooms

S:		£89
D:	£110 - £190	Suites: £190

The Royal Crescent

General Manager: **Ross Stevenson**

The Royal Crescent Hotel in Bath, part of the Cliveden collection, is situated in the centre of one of Europe's finest architectural masterpieces. Guests can enjoy Georgian splendour in the atmosphere of a private house, just a short stroll through historic streets or by a landscaped parkland walk to the city centre. Within the hotel are two restaurants, the Brasserie and Bar for stylish but informal dining and Pimpernel's in the mansion serving modern English cooking with a subtle Eastern influence, providing an intriguing range of dining experiences, with a walled garden offering the perfect environment for relaxed dining in the summer months.

The Bath House at The Royal Crescent, opening in July 1998, is a unique holistic spa offering an ambience of tranquillity. Among the many attractions that the hotel will be pleased to arrange are flights over the city and surrounding country in its own hot air balloon, and trips along the Kennet and Avon Canal on the Lady Sophina, a 1920's river launch.

Location: Central Bath

The Royal Crescent
16 Royal Crescent, Bath, Bath & NE Somerset BA1 2LS
Tel: 01225 823333   Fax: 01225 339401

45 rooms

D: £170 - £260   **Suites:** £370 - £675

Cliveden

Director and General Manager: **Stuart Johnson**

For three centuries Cliveden has been a house in which to entertain, and be entertained. Standing in 376 acres of the National Trust's finest parkland on a steeply wooded bend overlooking the River Thames, what was formerly one of Britain's most celebrated private residences is today one of its most highly rated hotels. The unique effect of the architecturally magnificent House, its beautiful setting, and the peerless hospitality and service provided by a complement of more than four staff per bedroom, combine to make Cliveden a truly unforgettable experience. The Terrace Dining Room, Michelin starred Waldo's restaurant, and renowned cellar have equally assured for Cliveden a worldwide reputation for culinary excellence.

The sports and leisure facilities are outstanding. The Pavilion garden is home to the outdoor pool (where Christine Keeler so notably met John Profumo), whilst the Pavilion itself houses an indoor pool, seven treatment and massage rooms, saunas, and a jacuzzi. There is also a fully equipped gymnasium, squash court, indoor and outdoor tennis courts, and horse riding in the grounds, with golf and shooting available nearby. During the summer months the hotel's three boats are available for cruising the Cliveden Reach of the River Thames.

Location: 23 miles west of London in Royal Berkshire

Cliveden, Taplow, Berkshire, SL6 0JF
Tel: 01628 - 668561   Fax: 01628 - 661837

Freephone: 0800 454063   Freefax: 0800 454064

38
rooms   **D:**   from £235   **Suites:**   from £425

The Bell Inn

Director and General Manager: **George Bottley**

The Bell Inn at Aston Clinton is an internationally acclaimed 17th century coaching inn whose original features provide a homely backdrop to the highly professional standards of service with which it helped establish the concept of the 'country house' hotel when it opened more than fifty years ago. The comfortable and attractive public rooms include the Writing Room and flagstoned Smoking Room: in the elegantly muralled restaurant classic French cuisine makes imaginative use of the best of seasonal and local produce, including Aylesbury duck specially bred for the The Bell Inn, stunningly served and complemented by a comprehensive wine list.

The individually styled bedrooms and suites, two with four poster beds, are situated either in the main house or around a cobbled courtyard, from the ground floors of which accommodation leads directly into the attractive gardens with its notable walled rose garden. Aston Clinton is attractively located, with Waddesdon Manor, Blenheim Palace, Hatfield House, and Woburn Abbey among the many sites of interest in the area.

Location: In the village of Aston Clinton on the A41 between Aylesbury and Tring

The Bell Inn, Aston Clinton, Buckinghamshire HP22 5HP
Tel: 01296 630252   Fax: 01296 631250

20 rooms

	S:	£60 – £130
	D:	£60 – £130

Scotland

For many centuries Scotland existed in the shadow of its southern neighbour, either in conflict or in staunch alliance. Yet few regions can boast the range of natural and human resources to which the country can lay so proud a claim.

In the Highlands and Islands, Scotland possesses a wilderness almost untouched by millennia of human occupation, and which made these rugged northern regions the last saving refuge of civilization during the bleak years of the Dark Ages. The central region offers a less austere landscape, the mountain peaks softened by lush valleys and salmon-rich rivers, while the great cities continue to display the energy and innovation which in former years placed them among the greatest powerhouses of Europe. Today, Scotland is reponding to the challenges of the modern world in the same way that its great thinkers and doers created so much of what we now take for granted in the world around us.

The visitor to Scotland will encounter a people fiercely and rightly proud of their history and heritage, the most important of which is a tradition of hospitality which includes the finest spiritous liquor known to man and an almost mystical respect for good food. From the Borders to the furthest islands, Scotland is a land of shared national character, and of unfailing surprise.

Month	Event	Venue
January		
January 25	Robert Burns Service and Wreath-Laying	St Michael's Church, Dumfries
January 31	Burns Night Celebrations	
February		
February 14	St Valentines Day Ski Race	Cairngorm Ski Area, Aviemore
February 14 - May 10	Exhibition: William MacTaggart	Scottish Gallery of Modern Art, Edinburgh
February 20 - March 21	Scotland's Dance Festival: Contemporary Dance	New Moves Centre for Contemporary Arts, Glasgow
February 21	Rugby International: Scotland v France	Murrayfield, Edinburgh
February 24 - March 1	Scottish Curling Finals	Perth Ice Rink, Perth
February - August	Exhibition: The Reformation in Scotland	St Mungo Museum, Glasgow
March		
March 22	Rugby International: Scotland v England	Murrayfield, Edinburgh
April		
April 3 - 5	Gleneagles Spring Show Jumping Festival	Auchterarder, Perthshire
April 9 - 12	Edinburgh Folk Festival	
April 18	Scottish Grand National	Ayr Racecourse, Ayr
April 24 - 26	Mull Music Festival	Tobermory
April 30 - May 4	Isle of Bute Jazz Festival	Rothsay and around the islands
May		
May 21 - 24	Orkney Folk Festival	Stormness, Orkney
May 21 - 31	Dumfries & Galloway Arts Festival	
May 22 - 31	Perth Festival of the Arts	
May 23 - 24	Atholl Highlanders' Parade and Gathering	Blair Castle, Blair Atholl
May 27 - June 2	Bergen - Shetland Yacht Race	Lerwick Harbour, Shetland Isles
May 29 - 31	St Fort Open Carriage Driving	St Fort, Newport-on-Tay
June		
June 25 - 28	Royal Highland Show	Ingliston Showground, Edinburgh
July		
July 8 - 11	Loch Lomond World Invitation Golf Tournament	Loch Lomond Golf Club
July 15 - 18	Hebridean Celtic Music Festival	Stornoway, Western Isles
July 17 - 26	Trossachs Highland Festival	Callander, Aberfoyle & Brig o'Turk
July 31 - August 1	Stirling Castle Concert	
August		
August 3 - 9	WPGA Golf Tournament	Gleneagles Hotel, Auchterarder
August 7 - 29	Edinburgh Military Tattoo	The Esplanade, Edinburgh Castle
August 9 - 31	Edinburgh Festival Fringe	
August 15	World Pipe Band Championships	Glasgow Green, Glasgow
September		
September 27 - 30	International Horse Trials & Country Fair	Blair Castle Gardens, Blair Atholl
September 5	Braemar Royal Highland Gathering	Princess Royal & Duke of Fife Memorial Park, Braemar
September 16 - 18	Ayr Gold Cup	Ayr Race Course
September 23 - 27	Oban Seafood Festival	Oban
October		
October 2 - 11	International Scotch Whisky Festival	Speyside & Edinburgh
October 8 - 11	Alfred Dunhill Cup	St Andrews
November		
November 5	Fireworks Extravaganza	Meadowbank Sports Stadium, Edinburgh
November 30	St Andrews Day	
December		
December 25	Men's & Boys' Ba' Games	Kirkwall, Orkney
December 26	Boxing Day Meeting	Ayr Racecourse, Ayr
December 28 - January 1	Hogmanay Celebrations	

ANTA

Fabrics and pottery

Distinctively Scottish.

Refreshingly original.

Created in the Highlands.

Available at our shop on the Royal Mile, or from our factory shop in Fearn

32 THE HIGH STREET • THE ROYAL MILE • EDINBURGH EH1 1TB   TELEPHONE 0131 557 8300
FEARN • TAIN • ROSS IV20 1XW   TELEPHONE 01862 832477   FAX 01862 832616

Country Quality

Brodie Countryfare is shopping with a distinctive difference. In a quiet and relaxed rural environment with ample parking, enjoy browsing in our wonderful gift department packed with original and exciting ideas in tableware, toys, interiors, soaps and candles, and stationery; and take your time to select from the wide range in Brodie Countryfare's famous clothing departments:

Countrywear   *country clothing for men and women*
Bubbles   *top ladies' fashion*
Hopscotch   *the best in children's designer labels*
Knitwear   *fine woollens and casual wear*

all brought to you with a traditional Scottish welcome and service. And if the sumptuous range of Scottish and world delicacies in the Food Hall sharpens your appetite, our traditional Scottish restaurant is open all day and provides the perfect end to a memorable shopping experience.

Brodie Countryfare
Brodie, by Forres
Moray
Scotland IV36 0TD

Telephone: 01309 641555
Facsimile: 01309 641499

OPEN SEVEN DAYS A WEEK

3 MILES WEST OF FORRES
ON THE A96

Brodie COUNTRYFARE

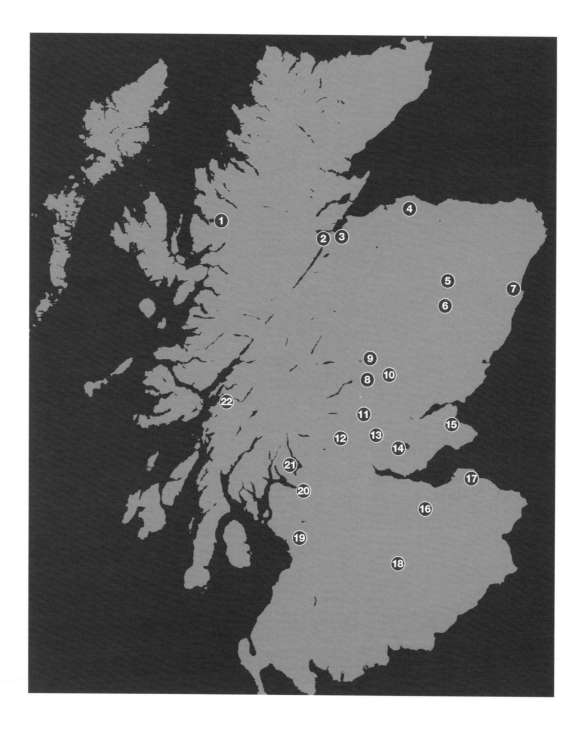

Loch Torridon Hotel

Proprietors: **David and Geraldine Gregory**

Once a grand shooting lodge built for the first Earl of Lovelace in 1887, Loch Torridon enjoys one of the most impressive coastal locations in the western Highlands. Set amidst 58 acres of mature parkland at the foot of Ben Damph, almost every window captures a unique aspect of the ever-changing mountain scenery.

The chance to walk, stalk, or fish in this unspoilt environment remains a powerful attraction, particularly where warm hospitality and excellent cuisine await at the end of the day. The hotel's extensive business facilities also provide a perfect opportunity for private and concentrated meetings and seminars in restful surroundings. A Scotland's Heritage Hotel

Location: Torridon is on the A896 west of Achnasheen

Loch Torridon Hotel, Torridon, by Achnasheen
Wester Ross IV22 2EY

Tel: 01445 791242 Fax: 01445 791296
E-mail: enquires@lochtorridonhotel.com

22 rooms

S: £85

D: £140

Suite: £250

Kingsmills Hotel

General Manager: **Iain Watson**

For centuries Kingsmills has stood in the ancient capital of the Highlands; as a mill for oatmeal, as a family home, and today as a spacious luxury hotel. The Kingsmills' 82 bedrooms include family rooms, rooms for the disabled, a sumptuous suite, and holiday villas in the landscaped grounds.

The Inglis Restaurant is highly regarded both locally and by hotel residents, with the finest of Scottish ingredients put to succulent and inventive use by the hotel's chefs. The Swallow Leisure Club is open for the enjoyment of all guests, and arrangements are available for a wide variety of sporting activities: a round on the adjacent golf course, fishing, clay pigeon shooting, horse riding, or mountain biking in the surrounding countryside. Business guests have the perfect excuse for enjoying the comforts of the Kingsmills, with three rooms catering for groups of up to 80 persons.

Location: One mile from Inverness town centre and a short drive off the A9

Kingsmills Hotel, Culcabock Road, Inverness IV2 3LP
Tel: 01463 237166 Fax: 01463 225208

82 rooms

S: £110

D: £155

Suite: £185

Culloden House

General Manager: Major Richard H Gillis

Situated within 40 acres of secluded parkland in the very heart of the Highlands, Culloden House is an imposing Georgian Grade A listed building which has retained much of its original architecture and features in accommodating a modern hotel with an emphasis on personal service and relaxation.

All bedrooms are individually styled and equipped to the highest expectation of modern comfort. During the summer a lone piper strides the grounds piping guests into The Adam Dining Room where Adamesque plasterwork, massive pillars and a large open fire provide a magnificent setting in which to enjoy the dishes prepared by the hotel's award-winning chef. Culloden House also offers excellent boardroom and conference facilities. A Scotland's Heritage Hotel.

Location: Three miles east of Inverness off the A96

Culloden House, Culloden, Inverness IV1 2NZ
Tel: 01463 790461 Fax: 01463 792181
E-mail: 106237.663@compuserve.com

28 rooms **S:** £135 **D:** £165 - £220 **Suites:** £240 - £250

Mansion House Hotel

Proprietors: Joan and James Stirrat

An imposing baronial house erected by the Bibby shipping line in beautifully landscaped grounds looking over the River Lossie, the Mansion House is a stone's throw from the centre of Elgin. The interior reflects the opulent tastes of the high Victorian era, with sumptuous detailing and extravagent individually-styled four poster bedrooms. Table d'hôte and à la carte menus are changed on a daily basis, taking best advantage of an extensive range of quality local produce to classical effect.

The Mansion House has a fully equipped country club, with swimming pool and gymnasium, and is an ideal base for investigating the natural beauties and distilleries of Speyside. A Scotland's Heritage Hotel

Location: Central Elgin

Mansion House Hotel, The Haugh, Elgin, IV30 1AW
Tel: 01343 548811 Fax: 01343 547916

23 rooms **S:** £75 **D:** £120 - £150 **Suites:** on request

Kildrummy Castle

Proprietors: **Thomas and Mary Hanna**

Set in the heart of the Grampian Highlands, Kildrummy Castle offers a rare opportunity to enjoy the style and elegance of a bygone era combined with all the comfort and service of a modern first class hotel. The award-winning restaurant specialises in the use of fresh local produce: Aberdeen Angus beef, fish and shellfish from the North Sea, and game from local estates.

The celebrated malt whisky distilleries of the Spey Valley and many of the North East's famous castles are a short distance from the hotel, while for the sportsman more than twenty golf courses, trout and salmon fishing, and horse riding can all be arranged in the vicinity. A Scotland's Heritage Hotel.

Location: Off the A97 35 miles west of Aberdeen

Kildrummy Castle, Kildrummy, by Alford, Aberdeenshire AB33 8RA
Tel: 019755 71288 Fax: 019755 71345

15 rooms
S: £75 - £80
D: £125 - £155

Darroch Learg Hotel

Proprietor: **Nigel Franks**

Darroch Learg stands in four acres of grounds on the wooded slopes above the picturesque village of Ballater. From its eminent position the hotel commands stunning views across Royal Deeside to the Grampian mountains.

The hotel has a relaxing country house style, with comfortable and elegant public rooms and individually furnished bedrooms. Five of these are in Oakhall, a baronial mansion situated in the grounds. The conservatory restaurant provides a delightful setting in which to enjoy the excellence of the food, which has been recognised by the award of three AA rosettes and the AA wine list of the year. A Scotland's Heritage Hotel.

Location: Ballater is approximately 42 miles west of Aberdeen

Darroch Learg Hotel, Braemar Road, Ballater
Aberdeenshire AB35 5UX
Tel: 013397 55443 Fax: 013397 55252
E-mail: darroch.learg@exodus.uk.com

18 rooms
S: £47.50
D: £95 - £115

The Marcliffe at Pitfodels

Proprietors: **Stewart and Sheila Spence**

Set in eight acres of woodland, the Marcliffe boasts forty-two bedrooms and suites mainly furnished with antiques brought from Invery House in Banchory. Two restaurants serve the finest of local and Scottish ingredients - the Conservatory Restaurant specialises in lobster and beef - supported by a vast cellar of over 400 bins augmented by the 130 whiskies and 60 cognacs available from the Drawing Room Bar.

The Marcliffe is affiliated to the Royal Aberdeen Golf Club, with nearby Cruden Bay also providing tee times. A wide range of activities can be arranged: hunting, stalking, shooting, off-road driving, and salmon and trout fishing. A member of Small Luxury Hotels of the World.

Location: Three miles west of the centre of Aberdeen on the A93

The Marcliffe at Pitfodels, North Deeside Road, Aberdeen AB15 9YA
Tel: 01224 861000 Fax: 01224 868860
E-mail: stewart@marcliff.win-uk.net

42 rooms

S: £135
D: £155
Suite: £195

Farleyer House

General Manager: **Andrew Cole**

As the principal residence of the head of the Clan Menzies, Farleyer House gained international renown for the exceptional warmth of its hospitality. Since becoming a hotel in 1989, the reputation of the house has been further enhanced by what has been described as among the most imaginative cooking in Britain. Its nineteen bedrooms, lounges and drawing rooms fully complement the standard of excellence rapidly established by The Scottish Bistro.

Hidden away in the spectacular Tay Valley, its 30 acres of grounds provide a wealth of quiet walks. For the more energetic, Farleyer House boasts some of the best fishing on the Tay as well as its own testing six-hole golf course, while guests may also enjoy membership facilities at the nearby Kenmore Country Club which include swimming, tennis, jacuzzi, sauna and sunbed. Private dining, board meeting, and seminar facilities are available for the business visitor.

Location: On the B846 approximately 40 miles north of Perth

Farleyer House Hotel, Aberfeldy, Perthshire, PH15 2JE
Tel: 01887 820332 Fax: 01887 829430
E-mail: andycole@compuserve.com

19 rooms

S: £90
D: £150
Suites: £180

Kinnaird

General Manager: **Douglas Jack**

Set in some of Scotland's most spectacular scenery, the handsome building which now houses the Kinnaird Hotel was built in 1770 as a dower house on the Atholl estate. In 1927 the house was bought by Lady Ward, whose daughter-in-law Constance converted it into a hotel in 1989. Preserving the special warmth and hospitality previously enjoyed by its house guests, the Kinnaird has rapidly taken its rightful place among the very top rank of our hotels.

Each of the nine bedrooms is uniquely designed and furnished to match the highest expectations of comfort, with massively accommodating beds and an open fire in most of the rooms. Magnificent trophy salmon in the billiard room attest to the proximity of the legendary Tay, a river which still commands fierce loyalty among salmon enthusiasts. A large yet surprisingly intimate drawing room leads into the elegantly panelled dining room, from which glorious views of Tayside add a unique lustre to a memorable culinary experience.

The quality of its cuisine is Kinnaird's crowning glory. The restaurant had won international acclaim within three years of the hotel's opening, and continues to attract both international recognition and an ever-growing army of grateful admirers.

Location: On B898 immediately north of Dalguise, approximately 22 miles north of Perth

Kinnaird, Kinnaird Estate, By Dunkeld, Perthshire PH8 0LB
Tel: 01796 482440 Fax: 01796 482289

9 rooms	**S:**	£80 – £110	
	D:	£235 – £295	**Suite:** £315

Ballathie House Hotel

General Manager: Christopher Longden

Built in 1850 in its own 1,500 acre estate overlooking the River Tay, Ballathie House offers Scottish hospitality in a setting of character and distinction. The original public rooms are elegantly furnished, and spacious master bedrooms retain antique furniture with period bathrooms featuring all modern facilities. The dining room has been awarded two AA rosettes, and features the pick of locally-produced ingredients.

Activities at Ballathie include fishing, tennis, croquet, putting and walking. The world-class golf courses at Rosemount, Carnoustie and St Andrews all lie within easy reach, with sufficient local courses to satisfy even the keenest golfer. A Scotland's Heritage Hotel.

Location: Approximately 10 miles north of Perth off A9 at Luncarty/Stanley turning: follow signs after Stanley.

Ballathie House Hotel, Kinclaven by Stanley
Perthshire, Scotland PH1 4QN
Tel: 01250 883268 Fax: 01250 883396
E-mail: email@ballathiehousehotel.com

28 rooms

| S: | £60 - £80 |
| D: | £120 - £180 |

Suites: £160 - £200

Auchterarder House

General Manager: Iain Russell-Jarvie

Built as a family home in 1832 and one of the finest Jacobean style country houses in Scotland, Auchterarder House is proud of its reputation as 'a special place'. Run with the informality of a home but to a standard of service expected of the world's top hotels, it is guided throughout by principles of privacy, intimacy, and personal service.

Fresh Scottish produce is presented with flair and imagination in the magnificent Victorian dining room. Bedrooms, each bearing the name of a clan, are individually different yet uniformly well appointed. Features throughout the hotel include open fires, many with unique fireplaces, oak panelling and crystal chandeliers, an expanse of books in the library and magnificent views of the Orchil and Grampian hills from the grounds that surround the house. Staff will be pleased to help arrange outdoor pursuits, with golf and fishing especially favoured. A member of the Wren's Hotel Group.

Location: Auchterarder is off the A824 between Stirling and Perth

Auchterarder House, Aucterarder, Perthshire, PH3 1DZ
Tel: 01764 663646 Fax: 01764 662939

15 rooms

| S: | from £120 |
| D: | from £160 |

Suites: from £180

Cromlix House

Proprietors: **David and Ailsa Assenti**

"Authentic excellence on an idyllic country estate": the beautiful and varied interiors of Cromlix House retain the historic ambience of a true ancestral home. Genuinely helpful staff provide a relaxed and hospitable introduction to its fourteen bedrooms (eight of them very large suites) and exceptional dining. House parties are welcomed, as are those wishing to arrange a wedding with a difference in its unique chapel.

In the vale of Strathallan north of Stirling, Cromlix provides a perfect base for relaxation or more extensive touring: Stirling Castle, distilleries and golf courses are all in the immediate vicinity, with Edinburgh, Glasgow and Perth within an hour's drive.

Location: On the B8033 approximately 8 miles north of Stirling

Cromlix House, Kinbuck, by Dunblane near Stirling,
Perthshire, FK15 9JT
Tel: 01786 822125 Fax: 01786 825450

14 rooms

S:	£95 - £125		
D:	£155 - £200	**Suites:**	£200 - £280

The Green Hotel

General Manager: **David JR McCulloch**

Formerly a 19th Century coaching inn, The Green is now an independently owned country house hotel with 47 spacious bedrooms all equipped to the highest standard.

Boasting a leisure complex with indoor pool, sauna, solarium, exercise facility and squash court, two all-weather tennis courts, two 18-hole golf courses with first tees a two minute walk from the front door, and a four sheet curling rink (in season), many will find all their holiday requirements within its extensive grounds. However, with Edinburgh, Glasgow, Stirling, St Andrew's, Perth, Pitlochry and the Perthshire Highlands less than an hour away, its central location also makes it the ideal touring centre for a family holiday or short break. A Scotland's Heritage Hotel.

Location: Kinross is half way between Edinburgh and Perth

The Green Hotel, 2 The Muirs, Kinross, KY13 7AS
Tel: 01577 863467 Fax: 01577 863180
E-mail: reservations@green-hotel.com

47 rooms

S:	£75		
D:	£125	**Suite:**	£130

Balbirnie House

Proprietors: **The Russell Family**

An outstanding Grade A listed Georgian country mansion set in a 400 acre estate, Balbirnie has been carefully restored as a privately owned and managed small luxury hotel providing an exceptional standard of service. Awarded 1996 Hotel of the Year by Taste of Scotland and the holder of four AA Red Stars, the warmth and quality of hospitality is a match for the distinctive grace and serenity of its period interiors.

Views from the house extend over well-manicured lawns and picturesque gardens to Balbirnie Park golf course, a satisfying 71-hole challenge. Balbirnie House's location makes it an ideal base for exploring the historic Kingdom of Fife, with St Andrews and Edinburgh both only a short drive away.

Location: Midway between Edinburgh and St Andrews off the A92 on the B9130

Balbirnie House, Balbirnie Park, Markinch, Glenrothes, Fife, KY7 6NE
Tel: 01592 610066   Fax: 01592 610529
E-Mail: Hotline.balbirnie@BTinternet.com

30 rooms

S:	£115	
D:	£170 - £210	Suites: £225

St Andrews Golf Hotel

Proprietors: **The Hughes Family**

Two stately Victorian houses in the celebrated town of St Andrews have been joined together to accommodate the St Andrews Golf Hotel. Interiors have been designed with taste and sensitivity which, combined with the dedicated efforts of the local staff, provides real Scottish hospitality - friendly, professional, but unobtrusive, with the comfort and convenience of guests always in mind.

The hotel enjoys breathtaking views over the links and St Andrews Bay, and is a mere hundred yards from the first tee of the Old Course. The historic Old Town of St Andrews lies a short walk away, with Dundee, Perth, and Edinburgh all within easy driving distance. A Scotland's Heritage Hotel

Location: Central St Andrews

St Andrews Golf Hotel, 40 The Scores, St Andrews, KY16 9AS
Tel: 01334 472611   Fax: 01334 472188
E-mail: thegolfhotel@standrews.co.uk

 22 rooms

S:	£81.50	
D:	£135 - £150	Suites: £170

Dalhousie Castle

Director: **Neville Petts**

For over 700 years Dalhousie Castle has been providing wholehearted Scottish hospitality from among the rolling Midlothian hills. Major restoration has woven modern comfort into the historic fabric of the pink sandstone walls whilst ensuring that elegant touches of the past remain. Fascinating reminders of a rich and turbulent history include the Dungeon Restaurant, a delightful setting in which to enjoy classical French and traditional Scottish 'Castle Cuisine'.

Eight of the twenty-nine bedrooms are historically themed and include the Robert the Bruce and Queen Victoria. Sumptuous fabrics and furnishings give the rooms an exclusive feel and the new 'de Ramseia' Suite houses the Castle's original well in the sitting room.

Five additional bedrooms with en-suite shower are available in the nearby 100 year old Lodge, situated in the original Castle Quarry. Just two minutes walk from the Castle, the Lodge has been refurbished in a relaxing country house style and overlooks the meandering South Esk River.

Five function rooms are available for banquets, weddings, meetings and international conferences, accommodating up to 120 guests or delegates, with a private helicopter landing site allowing high speed access.

Many outdoor activities can be arranged and local attractions include Edinburgh Castle, the Royal Mile and the Palace of Holyrood.

Location: 7 miles from Edinburgh city centre on the B704 between the A7 and A6094

Dalhousie Castle, Bonnyrigg, Edinburgh EH19 3JB
Tel: 01875 820153 Fax: 01875 821936
E-mail: res@dalhousiecastle.co.uk
Web site: www.dalhousiecastle.co.uk

34 rooms

S: from £70
D: from £90   **Suites:** from £160

The Open Arms

Proprietors: **Tom and Emma Hill**

Overlooking Dirleton's 13th Century castle on the southern shore of the Firth of Forth, The Open Arms offers the discreet comforts of a country house just 25 minutes from the heart of Edinburgh. With ten bedrooms individually furnished in classic style, lounges and cocktail bars warmed with log fires, and an award winning restaurant incorporating fresh local produce to innovative effect, the hotel is ideal for a relaxing break.

The Open Arms is located in the heart of golfing country amid an area of great historical and natural interest, with several sites of international ornithological importance within easy reach. A Scotland's Heritage Hotel

Location: *Off A198 between Gullane and North Berwick*

The Open Arms, Dirleton, East Lothian, EH39 5EG
Tel: 01620 850241 Fax: 01620 850570

10 rooms

S:	£75
D:	£60 - £75

Cringletie House

General Manager: **Charles Cormack**

Built in 1861 among the peaceful border hills near Peebles, Cringletie House is set in extensive grounds which include a croquet lawn, putting green and tennis court and a two acre walled garden. All rooms, including the thirteen well-appointed bedrooms, enjoy fine views of the surrounding landscape, in a hotel which takes pride in providing modern luxury in a traditional country house setting. Proud of its reputation for good food, fruit, vegetables and honey from the garden are among the fresh ingredients used to imaginative effect on a daily-changing menu.

Ideally situated for exploring the historic border towns along the Tweed Valley and with the attractions of Edinburgh a short drive away, fourteen golf courses can be reached within an hour's drive. Hotel staff will be happy to organise a permit for trout or salmon fishing on the Tweed. A member of the Wren's Hotel Group

Location: Set off the A703 between Eddleston and Peebles approximately 15 miles south of Edinburgh.

Cringletie House, Peebles, EH45 8PL
Tel: 01721 730233 Fax: 01721 730244

13 rooms

S:	£60
D:	£100

Montgreenan Mansion House Hotel

Proprietor: **Darren Dobson**

Set in 50 acres of secluded parkland and gardens, the mansion was built in 1817 and still displays the impressive architecture and decorative features of the period. Montgreenan is family owned and managed and prides itself both on its high standards of personal service and the genuine warmth of its hospitality. A six course table d'hôte dinner and à la carte menus are available daily, complemented by a fine cellar.

Close to Glasgow and Ayr, places of interest nearby include Culzean Castle, the Burrell Collection and Burns Cottage. Montgreenan is surrounded by a wealth of golfing attractions, with Old Prestwick and Royal Troon among the thirty top courses located within a 45 minute drive. A Scotland's Heritage Hotel

Location: Approximately 20 miles south west of Glasgow on A736

Montgreenan Mansion House Hotel
Kilwinning, Ayrshire KA13 7QZ
Tel: 01294 557733 Fax: 01294 850397
E-mail: Montgreenan.mansion@virgin.net

21 rooms

| S: | £75 |
| D: | £110 |

The Devonshire Hotel

General Manager: **Jeanette Montgomery**

Set in the West End of Glasgow only minutes from the many attractions of the city centre, the Devonshire offers a haven of peaceful seclusion in one of Europe's most exciting cities. Amid carved oak staircases, tastefully subdued lighting and stained glass, visitors are assured of individual service and a traditional style of hospitality.

From the intimate dining room for guests only, serving classical cuisine to a superb standard, to each of the fourteen individually-decorated and furnished en suite bedrooms, the Devonshire bespeaks quality and luxury throughout. The perfect location for a city and country holiday, with Loch Lomond an easy twenty minutes drive from the hotel and Edinburgh only forty five minutes by train, a warm welcome is guaranteed at the end of every trip.

Location: Off A82 approximately 2 miles north of Glasgow city centre

The Devonshire Hotel, 5 Devonshire Gardens, Glasgow G12 0UX
Tel: 0141 339 7878 Fax: 0141 339 3980
E-mail: Devonshir5.aol.com

14

| S: | from £100 | | |
| D: | from £120 | Suites: | from £150 |

Cameron House

General Manager: Roddy Whiteford

Cameron House stands on the southern shores of Loch Lomond, looking out across its waters towards majestic hills. Occupying over a hundred acres of woodland, and once the ancestral home of the illustrious Smollett family, today it provides the magnificent and inspirational focus of a luxurious hotel with an international reputation for the highest standards of service.

Owned and managed by the respected De Vere Group, Cameron House is widely acknowledged as one of the UK's finest leisure resorts, offering deluxe accommodation, excellent dining including the award-winning Georgian Room and stylish Smolletts, and superb sports and leisure facilities.

Cameron House has its own exclusive Leisure Club boasting some of the finest indoor leisure facilities in the whole of Scotland. The Estate also features a nine-hole golf course and its own marina – a perfect base from which to explore the numerous secluded beaches and islands of Loch Lomond.

Cameron House is set amidst the rich diversity of Scotland's heartland. To the east are Rob Roy country, the Trossachs, Stirling Castle

and Loch Katrine: to the north west lie the great sea lochs and the gateway to the Western Highlands. For a day in the city, the shops, museums and galleries of Glasgow are a mere twenty five miles away.

Location: Off the A82 northwest of Glasgow between Balloch and Luss

Cameron House Hotel & Country Estate, Loch Lomond, Dumbartonshire G83 8QZ
Tel: 01389 755565 Fax: 01389 759522

96 rooms

S: £135 – £145
D: £170 – £185   **Suites:** £275 – £385

Invercreran Country House Hotel

Proprietors: The Kersley Family

From its eyrie in the hills north of Oban, Invercreran commands one of the most sensational mountain views in Scotland. With all the facilities of a top class country house hotel, it has won a deserved reputation for the luxury of its bedrooms, the quiet comfort of its drawing rooms and the award-winning excellence of the cooking served in its terrace restaurant.

The mountains of the western Highlands and the inner Hebrides enjoy worldwide renown for their majesty and ever-changing beauty. Invercreran provides the ideal base for touring this area of unspoilt splendour, with your hosts always ready to answer your needs and provide the best in highland hospitality. A Scotland's Heritage hotel.

Location: Off the A828 between Oban and Ballachullish

Invercreran Country House Hotel, Glen Creran, by Oban, Argyll, PA38 4BJ
Tel: 01631 730414 Fax: 01631 730532
E-mail: invercreran@dial.pipex.com

9
rooms

S: £70
D: £150

Suite: £200

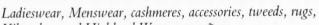

Ireland

Ireland is one of those strange regions which exist almost as strongly in the imagination as in reality. Most visitors to this beautiful land bring with them a weighty baggage of received ideas that are as unavoidable as they are misplaced.

In truth, Ireland is both much more and much less than its popular conception. Dublin may still and will forever be the city of a garrulous and hospitable race like no other, yet it is also a thriving European centre of commerce, finance and industry whose natives have for centuries used their carefully guarded public persona to mask one of the shrewdest business senses on earth. Rural Ireland may beguile with its much vaunted charm and simplicity, but be sure that even the apparently most rustic inhabitant possesses an awareness of place and perspective that the majority of us have lost many generations past. The Northern Ireland of the newsreels is a place of checkpoints and armed patrols, whereas the visitor will find few such unwelcome intrusions into a tour of one of Northern Europe's most breathtakingly beautiful regions.

There is only one precaution that the first time visitor to this magical land must always take, and that is to strip away all preconceptions and be prepared for the unexpected. In Ireland, it is usually just around the next bend.

Month	Event	Venue
January		
January - September	Salmon and Sea Trout Season	
February		
February 7	Rugby International Ireland v Scotland	Lansdowne Road, Dublin
February 23 - March 14	Belfast Music Festival	
March		
March 1-8	Arklow Music Festival	Arklow, Co Wicklow
March 3-12	Dublin Film Festival	
March 6- September 6	Exhibition of Dutch and Flemish 17th Century Art	Ulster Museum
March 17	St Patricks Day	
March 21	Rugby International Ireland v Wales	Lansdowne Road, Dublin
March 23 - April 5	Feis Ceoil, Classical Music Festival	Dublin
April		
April 4-11	World Championships in Irish Dancing	Ennis, Co Clare
April 11-14	Kerry Arts Festival and the Pan Celtic Festival	Tralee, Co Kerry
April 25-26	City of Belfast Spring Flower Show	Malone House
May		
May 7-10	Kinsale International Vintage Classic Car Rally,	Kinsale, Co. Cork
May 23	Belfast Civic Festival and Lord Mayor's Show	Belfast
May 29 - June 1	Castlebar Blues Festival	Castlebar, Co. Mayo
June		
June 26 - July 5	Ballybunion International Batchelor Festival	Ballybunion, Co Kerry
June 26-28	Maracycle, cycle ride between the two cities	Belfast and Dublin
June 26-28	Irish Derby Weekend	The Curragh Racecourse, Co Kildare
July		
July 2-5	Irish Open Golf Championship	Druid's Glen, Co Wicklow
July 10-13	Tour de France	Dublin and Cork
July 11-17	Sailing Regatta	Crosshaven, Co Cork
July 13	Ulster Derby	Down Royal, Co Down
July 31- Aug 3	Galway Races Summer Meeting	
August		
August 2-3	National Traction Engine Steam Rally,	Stradbally, Co Laois
August 2-9	Belfast Folk Festival	
August 5-9	Dublin Horse Show	RDS Showgrounds, Ballsbridge, Dublin
August 21-27	Rose of Tralee International Festival	Co Kerry
August 23	Mullaghmore Sea Angling Club Shark Safari	Co Sligo
September		
September 3-6	Jazz and Blues Festival	Monaghan
September 13	All-Ireland Hurling Festival	Croke Park, Dublin
September 1 -October 5	Lisdoonvarna Matchmaking Festival	Co Clare
September 24-27	Galway International Oyster Festival	
September 27	All Ireland Football Championship Final	Croke Park, Dublin
September 29	National Ploughing Championships	Ferns, Co. Wexford
October		
October 11-18	Cork Film Festival	
October 15 - November 1	Wexford Opera Festival	
October 23-26	Cork Jazz Festival	
November		
November 13-29	Belfast Festival at Queen's University	
December		
December 5-6	Dublin Antiques and Fine Arts Fair	
December 26	St Stephen's Day	

The Merrion

General Manager: **Peter MacCann**

From its opening in October 1997 the city's newest five-star hotel staked its claim to stand among the finest hotels in Europe. Occupying four magnificent terrace houses in the historic centre of Dublin, The Merrion restored these landmark buildings to their original Georgian grace and elegance with public and private rooms sympathetically decorated in period colours and styles, invisibly embellished by state of the art technology to ensure the optimum comfort and convenience of guests. The hotel also boasts one of Ireland's most important private art collections, carefully selected to complement each other and the classical elegance of the interiors and hung throughout the public areas for the enjoyment of all guests.

There are two restaurants and two bars: the renowned Restaurant Patrick Guilbaud, now in spectacular new premises; more informal dining in The Mornington Restaurant; The Cellar Bar, in the atmospheric setting of the original vaulted wine cellars; and No 23, a smaller more intimate cocktail bar. Landscaped period gardens provide a relaxing extension to the drawing rooms in warmer weather, with The Tethra Spa and its 18-metre pool open to all guests with health and fitness in mind.

Location: Central Dublin, opposite Government Buildings.

The Merrion, Upper Merrion Street, Dublin 2
Tel: 01 603 0600   Fax: 01 603 0700   E-mail: info@merrionhotel.ie

145 rooms

S: IRE £190 – £230
D: IRE £210 – £255   **Suites:** IRE £350 – £650

The Park Hotel, Kenmare

Proprietor: **Francis Brennan**

The renowned Park Hotel Kenmare possesses an ambience that has more in common with a private home filled with friends than that traditionally associated with a hotel. Immediately on entering open fires and fresh floral displays in the public areas, and the warm welcome from the host Francis Brennan, put the visitor at ease. All of the private rooms are equally and grandly accommodating, making use of fine furnishings and designed with space and comfort uppermost in mind, all with marble bathrooms. Suites and superior rooms command spectacular views over the eleven acres of landscaped garden terraces to the ever-changing vista of Kenmare Bay.

The hotel's elegant Dining Room has won numerous awards and accolades for both its service and cuisine: Hotel of the Year 1997, Condé Nast Best Hotel, and three AA rosettes being some of the most recent recognitions of its excellence. A tennis court, croquet lawn, fitness suite and adjoining 18 hole golf course provide physical stimulus for active guests, while the hotel is situated on the famous Ring of Kerry scenic route, opening up the magnificent mountain and coastal scenery and historic sites of the Iveragh Peninsula - Ireland's Lake District.

Location: Kenmare is 21 miles south of Killarney on the N71

The Park Hotel Kenmare, Kenmare, County Kerry
Tel: 064 41200   Fax: 064 41402   E-mail: phkenmare@iol.ie

50 rooms

S: IRE £120
D: IRE £220 - £316   **Suites:** IRE £370

Dromoland Castle

Group General Manager: **Mark Nolan**

Dromoland Castle, ancestral seat of the High King Brian Boru, is today a luxurious five-star hotel set in 375 acres of private parkland with a lake and its own 18 hole golf course. In a setting of spectacular splendour and romance the hotel offers up-to-date facilities for the most discerning traveller, ensuring a unique experience for all visitors. The 75 sumptuously designed bedrooms, the majority commanding magnificent views over the park or lake, are the work of the internationally renowned interior designer Carol Roberts, of "No. 12 Queen St" Bath, who carefully selected only the finest Irish materials to complement the stone and wooden fabric and beautiful casement windows of the Castle. The family portraits adorning the walls and open log fires establish a warm welcome and enhance the elegant comfort of the five public rooms.

The restaurant has been voted the best in Ireland: rich Victorian wall hangings harmonise with the original woodwork and offset tables covered with Irish linen and laid with Wicklow silver, Cavan crystal, and Wedgewood china, all overlooking the beautiful Lough Dromoland. A mere fifteen minutes from Shannon Airport, the local area is especially favoured for fishing, golf, riding and shooting, with a wealth of historic attractions within easy reach.

Location: Eight miles north of Shannon Airport off the N18

Dromoland Castle, Newmarket-on-Fergus, County Clare
Tel: 061 368144   Fax: 061 363355   E-mail: sales@dromoland.ie

75 rooms   **D:**   from IRE £220   **Suites:** to IRE £700

Ashford Castle

Managing Director: Rory Murphy

On the shores of Lough Corrib and a living Irish legend dating back to the 13th century, Ashford Castle is surely one of the most romantic hotels in the world. Its 83 luxury bedrooms and suites, most of which enjoy breathtaking views of the lake and the Cong River on which St Patrick sailed, have recently been refurbished with such success that Ashford has been voted fourth among the World's Best Hotels and Best Hotel in Ireland for the past seven years in succession. The renovated interiors of the Castle have meticulously retained their original historic features, most notably the superb gallery with hand-carved bannister rail which overlooks the Main Hall and the dramatic inglenook fireplace which stretches from the floor to the 20ft ceiling in the retiring room. The sumptuously panelled George V Dining Room offers an intriguing variety of continental and traditional dishes, while the Connaught Room serves classic French cuisine in a warm and intimate environment.

A 9-hole private golf course, Equestrian Centre, and fishing on the lake and rivers on the estate complement the wealth of sporting activities available in the locality. Ashford is an hour and a half's drive

from Shannon Airport through beautiful countryside, in a region renowned in history and legend.

Location: Twenty seven miles north of Galway off the R346

Ashford Castle, Cong, County Mayo
Tel: 092 46003   Fax: 092 46260   E-mail: ashford@ashford.ie

83
rooms

S: IRE £220

D: IRE £220   **Suites:**   IRE £475

Glenlo Abbey

General Manager: Philip Ryan

Formerly home to the Ffrench and Blake families, two of the fourteen tribes which for centuries ruled Galway, the 18th century Glenlo Abbey opened as a luxury hotel in 1992, and is now Galway's only five-star hotel, AA Red Star, and holder of the RAC Blue Ribbon. Bedrooms and suites are exquisitely furnished with an emphasis on generous space and comfort, and several afford wonderful views over Lough Corrib. Public rooms, which include the River Room restaurant and the Oak Cellar Bar, reflect the same meticulous attention to modern convenience blended with warmth and character in their restoration of the historic fabric of the abbey.

The estate is also home to a 1920's Pullman train which has been converted into a restaurant and cocktail bar. Their carriages were formerly part of the original Orient Express and are famous not only for their style and elegance but also for the renowned personages they carried, among them Sir Laurence Olivier and Sir Winston Churchill.

Glenlo Abbey is tucked away on a 138-acre waterfront golf estate. Guests can enjoy fishing, lake-boating, and clay pigeon shooting on site, while the vibrant city of Galway is a mere five minutes away by car.

Location: Two and a half miles north of Galway on the N59.

Glenlo Abbey Hotel, Bushypark, Galway
Tel: 091 526666   Fax: 091 527800   E-mail: glenlo@iol.ie

46
rooms

S: from IRE £115
D: from IRE £155   **Suites:**   from IRE £300

New perspec

DATE DUE

8051

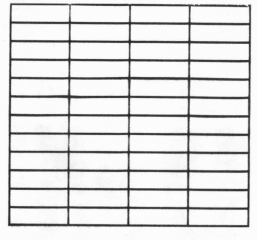

DEMCO

For further information
Ptarmigan Publishing Ltd
Growers Court
New Road
Bromham, Chippenham
Wiltshire SN15 2JA

Telephone: 01380 -859983
Facsimile: 01380 -859682

Printed by Sceptre Litho, Leicester